BORN TOO EARLY

BORN TOO EARLY
Hidden Handicaps
of Premature Children

Jonna Jepsen

Foreword by
Gorm Greisen

Translated by
Helen Martin

KARNAC

First published in 2006 by
Karnac Books
118 Finchley Road
London NW3 5HT

British Library Cataloguing in Publication Data

A C.I.P. for this book is available from the British Library

ISBN-13: 978-1-85575-354-9
ISBN-10: 1-85575-354-5

Printed in Great Britain

www.karnacbooks.com

This book is dedicated to my beloved children Filip and Marina,
who have fought so bravely,
and without whom I would not have my insight, interest,
and understanding

CONTENTS

ACKNOWLEDGEMENTS

During my work with this book I have received excellent help and support from professionals with knowledge, insight, will—and heart. I owe many thanks to these persons for their willingness, involvement, and professional appraisal:

— Gorm Greisen, paediatrician, professor, dr. med., Rigshospitalet, Copenhagen, for the paediatric part and for the Foreword;

— Hanne Agerholm, leading physiotherapist, Aalborg Sygehus Nord, for appraisal of the passages about physiotherapy and occupational therapy;

— Bo Moelholm, paediatrician, Rigshospitalet, Copenhagen, for contributing to the passage about the ETFOL study;

— Gideon Zlotnik, children's psychiatrist, for appraisal of passages about stress;

— Peter Uldall, children's neurologist, Rigshospitalet, Copenhagen, for appraisal of passages about the nervous system and the brain (it should be noted that Peter Uldall does not share all the author's views and opinions);

— Mette Andreassen, manager of the family and social services department, family therapist, Spoettrup, for contributing to the passages about social legislation and for an appraisal of the contents of the whole book;

— Inger Thormann, Skodsborg, and Inger Poulsen, Horsens, both infant therapists, for an appraisal of the passages about trauma and infant therapy;

— Lisbeth Skafte, nutritionist, Hvidovre Hospital, Copenhagen, for appraisal of the passages about nutrition and eating problems;

— Trine Rosenberg, cranio-sacral therapist, occupational therapist, Silkeborg, for appraisal of all passages about cranio-sacral therapy;

— Michael Cohrt, physiotherapist, osteopath, Lumsaas, for appraisal of the passage about osteopathy;

— Mona Lise Larsen, NLP therapist, Ballerup, for appraisal of the passage about NLP;

— Anne Marie Klysner Møller, neonatal nurse, Roskilde Amts Sygehus, for appraisal of the passages about nursing and for an overall appraisal of the book;

— Trine Boardman, child care worker, and Klavs Frisdahl, cand. com., both from Roskilde, for appraisal of the passages about child care and Holding therapy;

— Mie Andersen, cand.mag., Naestved, and Hanne Sigaard, school teacher, Viby, for an appraisal of the whole book.

(The five last-mentioned persons are all parents of premature children.)

— Finally also many thanks to the parents who through case studies have shared their sorrows and joys with us, and thus have brought all the theoretical conceptions alive.

FOREWORD

Gorm Greisen

Why was this book not written earlier? Why could Jonna Jepsen not find anything to refer to when she was asked where one could find information about all the problems that prematurely born children can run into later on in their lives?

In my opinion it is a matter of perspective.

As a parent, as an ardent person behind the Danish Society for Premature Children [*Dansk Praematur Forening*], as a lecturer to parents and to professionals within social services and health care, and through extensive reading Jonna Jepsen has achieved a unique perspective: one that focuses upon the pain caused by the disadvantaged start, the respect for the little miracle that every child is, and the will to find solutions to the problems. One cannot help being impressed by this, and I believe that this book written by her is very valuable. It shows what can be achieved through solid perseverance.

Gorm Greisen, dr.med., is a paediatrician and professor at Rigshospitalet, Copenhagen.

I think that the reason why a book such as this has not been written before is because no one coming from any other perspective could try to cover so many professional areas, be open to so many different information sources, and have such faith in the many and varied kinds of treatment.

The professional perspective is different. There is nothing called a "premature child doctor" or a "premature child-care worker". I personally work with premature children's problems in the period after their birth and until they can be discharged from the hospital. But I also work with illnesses in other newborn children. Other paediatricians work with children's handicaps or functional disorders, not especially with premature children's problems. Teachers and therapists are typically specialized in certain kinds of treatment. Therefore it would take a group of professionals to write this book—as a technical and scientific book.

There is a further difference in the perspectives. Although most professionals are convinced about the usefulness of their own endeavours, they can be sceptical about the usefulness of some of their colleagues' efforts. A treatment can be shown to be useful by means of a controlled study: one in which children who receive treatment are compared to children who do not receive treatment. If controlled studies show an effect, it is easier to convince other groups of professionals. Unfortunately, not many types of treatment have been tested by controlled studies, and therefore it has to be said that the use of a treatment often rests on faith.

However, from the parents' perspective it can be enough to believe that there is a chance that the treatment will be of use.

And that might be the most important question this book asks: How far to go? In rather brutal terms, the choice is between seizing every opportunity to treat, train, and improve—or accept, adjust oneself, and get the best out of the situation as it is. In less simple terms, the choice lies between striving to help and simple acceptance.

That is a choice for all parents of children who began life with a disadvantaged start. As professionals, we have to be ready to support the parents in the choices they make.

PREFACE

During the past few years I have often been asked whether I could recommend a book about typical late consequences of pre-term birth. I could not do that, so I decided to make an attempt to fill that void.

During the work with the book I have constantly been under the influence of impressions that remain stamped on my memory: stories about, and observations of, premature children and their families who have been referred to me during my lectures and my teaching, which consists of in-service training of, among others, day-care and child-care workers, teachers, special teachers, nurses, and health visitors. At the lectures and through the work in the Danish Society for Premature Children, many parents of premature children have told me stories from real life showing the huge difficulties, great frustrations, and lack of understanding, support, and help. My own personal experiences with extremely premature twins through 11 years have been a solid foundation for a deeper understanding. Masses of literature have placed the experiences in a more theoretical perspective.

I am convinced that the lack of understanding, support, and help that many families experience is *not* caused by a lack of will but, rather, by lack of knowledge and insight on the part of those who have been in close contact with the families.

Why should it be that premature children and their families often have huge problems for which they cannot receive help and support?

And why is a book like this needed, particularly when we have a follow-up system within the social services and in the health care area?

The typical difficult-to-discern consequences of premature birth lie within the areas represented by the senses, motor control, mentality, emotions, and interaction—that is, the psychological, psychosocial, social-pedagogical, and sensorimotor functional areas. In Denmark, follow-up control of prematurely born children is mainly taken care of by paediatricians, who traditionally do not work within these areas.

This can mean that many premature children who get an "acquittal" when discharged after a long follow-up period at the children's outpatient clinic will have to live on with problems that have not been identified. However, it has to be said that in some municipalities premature children are referred to a physiotherapist or an occupational therapist at an early stage. The follow-up efforts of the social services and the health care units differ a great deal and are dependent on local expert knowledge. Many parents find that they themselves have to seek information and insight, draw attention to the child's disabilities, explain and defend, initiate treatments outside the established system, coordinate the various efforts, follow up, and be in the lead.

A report published by the Danish government health service on the future organization of neonatology (Sundhedsstyrelsen, 1994) states:

> Follow-up investigations at school age of children with very low birth weight has shown that in addition to the [previously] stated actual handicaps, there is a major group of children with school problems, behavioural problems, etc., who are in need of special support throughout the school period.
>
> The social and economic conditions of the families have a considerable influence on the extent of these problems. This large group of premature children and their families need active support during the children's years of growth and the school period. That includes long maternity leave, motor func-

tional training, and a special psychological and pedagogical effort, both at the preschool age and during the school period.

Premature children suffering consequences of their early birth do not grow out of them, and new difficulties may appear as the children mature. The individual traumatic and stressing experiences are not, by themselves, the greatest threat to the child's healthy mental condition and good quality of life. The sum of negative influences from the time in the NICU (Neonatal Intensive Care Unit), eventual problems with interaction, and, later, a defective or delayed development can cause continuous problems for premature children. But the children can be protected if we initiate the necessary support. A parent or other carer of a child with mental, emotional, and other developmental difficulties will have no doubt that the child needs help. Exactly in the same way as no one will fail to set a fractured arm, so no one should fail to help a child with difficulties of a less discernible kind. As a community we have decided to initiate treatment and to save the life of infants born several months before term, and therefore we also have an obligation to offer the children the support that they might need throughout their years of growth.

An early effort can prevent the typical consequences of preterm birth, so that the children will have quite a normal childhood. If the minor difficulties are identified, it is possible to take care of them before they develop into huge problems.

Therefore, throughout the children's years of growth it is important for both parents and professionals to be aware of the children's development—not in an anxious and worrying way, but by calm observation, knowing that it is possible to rectify imbalances.

And that is just the purpose of this book: to give parents and professionals close to the child a possibility to prevent, repair, and rebuild. And it is my hope that parents of premature children will find in this book support to trust their own feelings, sensations, strength, and competence.

Even though a large group of premature children will have to face the consequences of a birth that came too early, we must be aware that premature children are just as much individuals as are all other children, and that some of them are therefore more robust, healthy, and strong-willed than others, as well as that the children's inborn temperament and individuality has an influence on their ability to master and manage things in life. We must be happy about the conquests of neonatology and the ability of the children's mental and physical strengths, the follow-up system, and the parents to repair and rebuild. And we must rejoice in the strength and power that little infants take with them further in life, having survived such a harsh and dangerous start. And at the same time, we will continuously have to be aware of the need to help and support the many children who are born too early every year, and who might suffer consequences because of that. The older children and adolescents who today live with the consequences of too early a birth also need attention.

The structure of the book

The book deals not with the more usual handicaps but exclusively with the less visible consequences of pre-term birth, which are seldom diagnosed. ADHD and epilepsy are seen more frequently among premature children than among children born at term, and autism in particular shows up among children who are born before Gestational Week 27. These are conditions that can be related to brain dysfunctions and are possible to diagnose.

There are border areas—such as, for example, sensory shyness, fearlessness (bravado), and "lack of social filter"—but these have been omitted as they belong to the minor part of the consequences of pre-term birth and can also be caused by other circumstances.

The book describes the causes of the consequences of pre-term birth; the possible consequences are explored point by point with identification of causes, and the possible ways of rectifying or ameliorating these are listed. It also details possibilities for prevention, support, and treatment as well as the need for public support arrangements.

For an explanation of the technical terms used, a Glossary is provided at the end of the book.

BORN TOO EARLY

CHAPTER ONE

The disadvantaged start

A child is born too early when it is born before the end of the 37th week of pregnancy. Very premature children arrive in the world before the end of the 32nd week, and extremely premature babies are those who see the light of the day before the end of the 28th week.

In order to establish categories—for research purposes, for example—the three groups above are defined by weight limits of 2,500 g, 1,500 g, and 1,000 g, respectively.

Weight is not of significant relevance for the premature child's chances of survival and risk of hidden, or delayed, handicaps. However, the child's maturity plays a major role, and this is directly related to the week of birth. The lungs, as well as the brain and the maturity of the nervous system, are particularly significant factors in relation to delayed handicaps.

The degree and range of inflicted stress and painful treatment are also deciding factors for both the possibility of complications in the neonatal period and consequences in the longer term.

The time-span of separation between mother and child, together with the extent of painful and unpleasant nursing and treatment, are crucially important to how traumatized the premature child will become.

The life-force the child displays immediately after birth is a very significant factor in the child's survival chances and ability to survive through the hospitalization period without serious complications.

Children born at term may also be exposed to separation, growth retardation, shock, or fear/pain in connection with operations or other treatment, and they may in these circumstances display some of the same characteristics as those seen in prematurely born children.

The child's experience of a pre-term birth

There is broad agreement among psychologists of the newborn that the first two years of the child's life are particularly important for the development of personality. However, newer research does show that it is always possible to carry out repairs to mental imbalance created early in childhood (Schaffer, 1990).

Being born is a violent, shocking experience, and the shock is substantially worse when this happens much too early, partly because the child is totally unprepared, partly because the birth and following examination and treatment usually take place in a stress-filled acute environment.

Children who arrive in the world much too early are generally delivered by Caesarean section, removed immediately from the mother, examined, placed into an incubator, and taken to the Neonatal Intensive Care Unit (NICU). Alone in the world, away from the only secure place they know: mother's protective body, her smell, voice, and heartbeat. Their next experience is to have a probe inserted, be pricked with a needle, have electrodes attached, and be placed into a CPAP (Continuous Positive Airway Pressure) device or respirator.

The children cannot express their shock, fear, and pain and that is precisely why the experience is extra traumatic.

Separation from the mother

The child experiences and registers separation from the mother as a privation and a deep feeling of betrayal, which the child may harbour for a long time if nothing is done to prevent it. Many prematurely born children have an (unconscious) deep feeling of anger against their mother, which may be expressed by, for example, rejection of comforting and caresses.

Results of several investigations carried out during the last five decades indicate that there is a causal connection between loss of maternal care in early childhood and disturbed development of personality (Bowlby, 1969–80).

The premature child's traumatic start in life stands in sharp contrast to the full-term infant's entry into the world:

The mother's care and presence after the birth guarantees the child's physical and mental survival. In the postnatal period—that is, the first weeks after a full-term birth—the child sleeps much of the time, is nursed, fed, and given warmth and security. It experiences the maternal rhythmic heartbeat during feeding and when it is carried. In this condition of total satisfaction of all needs, where milk and the feeling of being securely held by, and being at one with, the mother is present in unlimited amounts, the child achieves trust in itself and in its mother. With this satisfaction of all the child's needs, the requirements for development of the basic trust are fulfilled and emotionally solid and safe foundations for the child's development are laid.

If the infant loses—or is deprived of—bodily contact with the mother, this can give rise to an existential fear in the child. The Swiss ethnologist Franz Renggli calls bodily contact "the universal calming medicine" for babies.

According to the child analyst Margaret Mahler, the child develops a weak "self" as a result of early separation, and it becomes vulnerable and frightened (Mahler, Pine, & Bergman, 1975). The influence of early separation on the child must be judged in connection with factors described below under "Pain and unfulfilled needs", "Stress", and "Parent–child interaction". When the child is exposed to pain and stress and is at the same time separated from its secure base, the mother, these influences reinforce its fears.

Pain and unfulfilled needs

At very early birth children's organs are immature, which means that they cannot breathe independently, eat, maintain their temperature, or resist infections. In short, they cannot survive without either use of the kangaroo method (child and parent, skin against skin) 24 hours a day, which is not used in the NICU's, or intensive technological and medicinal intervention.

This intensive treatment means that in the first, acute phase the child is touched some 100 times every 24 hours, and later, during the neonatal progress, 70 times during the day and night (Ulvund, Smith, Lindemann, & Ulvund, 1992). Most often it is painful and unpleasant contact, carried out by many different hands. Blood samples are generally taken by means of a cut with a scalpel in the child's heel. When a drip has to be inserted for delivery of medicine or glucose, it can be difficult to hit the hair-fine veins, and not infrequently it is necessary to puncture the skin several times before success is achieved.

If the mucous membranes are undamaged, it does not markedly hurt the child to have a probe put in place, but it is very unpleasant.

A very premature child has a parchment-thin skin and experiences pain more intensely than does a full-term child. A premature child will, at Week 28, react to a pressure on the skin of 0.25 g, whereas a full-term child will ignore pressure of less than 1.8 g. The number of pain receptors (nerve endings) is highest at a birth age of 28 weeks, and it is considered that at this time the child is unable to inhibit the pain impulse. So, the lower the age at birth, the greater the pain (Sørensen, 2001, pp. 11–13).

Children born extremely early, who are exposed to much pain, also become the victims of the phenomenon *hyperalgesia:* the child experiences the same stimulation as being more and more painful each time. Eventually the sensitive child's nervous system can register just a touch as pain.

The preliminary results of research in this field indicate that there is a better prognosis in relation to neurological damage in children who are protected against pain during a course of treatment than in children who are treated without this added protection (Sørensen, 2001, p. 27).

The pain suffered in the period of infancy by children born too early is probably the reason why most of them can later bear much pain. They have become hardened. But stress can also be contributory to the development of a high pain threshold (Zlotnik, 2001), and as pain and situations of fear connected with this give rise to stress, there could be a connection between early experienced pain, stress, and a raised pain threshold.

The CPAP-system, which assists the child with breathing, blows a continual stream of air into the nose, and the child experiences this as a continuous, high blowing sound very close by. This, and other sounds, are enhanced in the closed Perspex incubator.

The child is often awakened for examination, treatment, or feeding, just as it may waken when the many alarms in the NICU are activated.

For the very premature child, despite the fact that more and more protective nursing and treatment methods are implemented, these negative stimuli, in the shape of painful treatment and unpleasant handling, are everyday experiences. When the child's initial experiences of life and with other people are very negative, a fundamental fear is created: fear of new things, of new places, of strange people—yes, virtually everything that is new or strange.

An infant who does not have its needs satisfied during a disturbed development sequence or progress closes itself off from contact with the rest of the world in order to protect itself against the negative stimuli.

New research shows that a new-born, full-term baby can register or perceive threats and dangers against its existence. The child attempts to ward these off by means of evasive bodily manoeuvres in relation to the object that appears to come towards it. The child can mentally protect itself by freezing activity with simultaneous closure of sensory input and increased motor activity in combination with increased alertness.

But a child born too early has not developed any barriers to stimuli at birth. The child can sense and register the danger but does not have the resources to react to it or to shield itself from it.

Following an overloaded and frustrating infancy, unpleasant emotionally laden experiences are predominant, giving the child negative expectations with regard both to itself and to its surroundings and creating a fundamental insecurity.

When, after a such frustrating period of babyhood, the child has eventually built up a symbiosis with the mother, it often becomes fixated on this symbiosis and will not be able, like other children in the 5–36-month age-group, to tolerate separation and find its independence. The mother—and the father—supremely represent the child's secure base, and it can be quite difficult for the child to feel secure when together with others.

Stress

The concept of "stress" is not used in the daily clinical work with children, and there is little research into this area. However, a great deal of the knowledge gained about stress in adults can be transferred to children because it is related to general physiological processes (Zlotnik, 2001).

Nature's intention with the stress reaction is to prepare the organism for dangerous situations so they can be fought or avoided—that is, fight or flight. When the brain registers the danger, it sends messages, by way of the pituitary gland, to the adrenal glands to increase the production of hormones, particularly adrenalin and cortisone. The nervous system is activated, the blood pressure and the heart-beat rate are increased, the kidney function is reduced, the fat content of the blood is increased, blood sugar is increased, and extra blood is supplied to the muscles. The blood becomes thicker (coagulates slightly). These mechanisms increase people's physical capacity (in case of battle) and reduce bleeding (in case of wounding).

However, when stress thus places the body in a state of alert, other functions are reduced. Repair of muscle and bone tissue is slowed down, and risk of bleeding in the brain is increased.

Focus is on two types of stress in the scientific area:

— Type I stress in the shape of acute trauma or event;

— Type II stress in the shape of daily and long-term exposure.

Researchers consider that response to Type I stress exposure will be momentary and without long-term effect and that this type of stress is a normal, positive, or constructive form of stress.

To Type II stress exposure the reaction will be weighty, negative, or destructive. The organism will be in a continual state of alarm, and in this condition stress becomes *distress*, which can, in some cases, develop to become symptoms and illness, including, for example, allergies (Zlotnik, 2001). The immune system is strengthened by acute stress situations, but it is weakened by long-lasting exposure. Stress of longer duration and/or strong stress exposure is damaging not only for the body but also for the psyche.

Children born too early can be judged to be exposed to both types of stress in that they, after a period of acute trauma, often have to live for many years in a non-thriving state due to the consequences of birth and hidden handicaps.

The child born too early is more sensitive to and is influenced more by stress than is a full-term child. This is due to the immaturity of the brain and the nervous system, leading to a greater risk of mental and physical effects of stress.

The premature child is exposed to stress while still in the embryonic state, when conditions in the womb are not as they should be. When the expectant woman becomes aware that there are problems with the pregnancy, her fears and unease can create stress, and her enhanced stress-hormone levels will be transferred to the foetus.

If birth begins too early—often under dramatic circumstances—the next stress-filled experience is added. Thereafter the acute neonatal environment, the physical pain, the discomfort, the fear, the lack of security, and the separation are significant factors of stress. Additionally, the child's battle to overcome infection and to survive induces stress.

If the child is stressed early and frequently, a stress build-up will accumulate in the body, and the child will later need help to be rid of this. The more stress the body is exposed to, the more tense its muscles become.

Stress is an vicious cycle. The tense muscles make it difficult for the child to relax and fall asleep; it makes the digestive processes difficult, with accompanying pain and tears, and it increases the pain. This causes additional stress hormones to be produced and circulated in the body, and thus stress caused by external circumstances is strengthened by the child's own organism (Rosenberg, 2002b).

Research shows that children who are exposed to early stress have difficulty in mastering stress-filled situations later, just as they will be more predisposed to illness (Milsted, 1999).

When children are exposed to chronic stress, change can occur in parts of the brain. An underdeveloped brain will be more vulnerable and exposed. These structural changes may be partly the cause as to why the child may later have problems with registering and finding meaning in patterns of perception (problems with integration of the senses), and it can have influence on the child's short-term memory and learning ability.

As there is a connection between stress reaction and the natural growth hormones (Zlotnik, 2001), one must be aware of the influence of stress factors on premature children's frequently occurring growth problems.

Experience from a project at Amtssygehuset County Hospital in Glostrup, Denmark (Kirkebæk, Clausen, & Storm, 1996) indicates that premature children who are protected as much as possible against stress and overloading fare better, both mentally and physically, than do children where no special care has been taken in relation to stress loads as part of the neonatal care.

Parent–child interaction

The combined conditions described above may contribute to poor parent–child interaction. Both child and parents begin their acquaintance with a shock, followed by fear in both parties: for the parents, fear of losing their child and fear of the child being handicapped. Mothers of children born extremely early not uncommonly want no contact with their child because emotionally they want to protect themselves in case the child does not survive.

It is, additionally, difficult to have close and positive contact with each other partly because of the intensive care needed and the connected equipment, partly because of lack of time. When the child has to be frequently nursed and treated and has to rest in between, there is not much time left over for positive bonding.

One can say that these children's senses are over overstimulated, while they are emotionally understimulated.

It can be extremely difficult to interpret the premature child's weak signals, and therefore it can take a long time before the parents feel able to comprehend and anticipate the child's needs. An extended period during which the parents are unable to satisfy all the child's needs and may harbour a feeling of being incompetent parents may have a negative influence on the interaction between parent and child.

Health-care professionals involved with the family play a significant role in connection with the parents and their feelings, and they are in a position to influence and strengthen the parents' self-esteem and self-confidence.

Traumas and their consequences

Very premature and extremely prematurely born children, who undergo lengthy and intensive treatment and are separated from their parents for longer periods, are particularly likely to be burdened with traumas.

It is very important to emphasize here that the child's early experience of betrayal and injustice should not give knowledgeable, responsible, and caring parents and health-care professionals personal feelings of guilt. The parents' presence and love are of invaluable benefit to the child. Nowadays there is much effort made to avoid separation, as well as to lessen or prevent pain, and so on, and conditions in NICUs are continually improving. It must be remembered that the separation and the painful and unpleasant treatment is, to a certain extent, essential if the child is to survive.

Traumatized children avoid everything that is new and unknown. They withdraw entirely from the world—they shield themselves totally. They experience continual inner tension and increased watchfulness (stress).

These children regress in their relationship to their parents and become dependent on them in order to maintain their equilibrium.

They will have difficulty in developing an inner life, and their ability to develop through play and their capacity to use symbols, which through play represent experience, are reduced.

They may have incomprehensible outbursts of rage, often in connection with being exposed to situations that they want to avoid.

It is well known that traumas influence older children and adults, but we had not been aware that traumas also affect infants, partly because investigation into infants is a comparatively recent field of research.

Infants who are suffering hardship can arouse very strong feelings in adults—feelings against which we intuitively guard ourselves. To avoid the anguish of seeing the child's suffering, we adults often experience a need to forget, and this can be a hindrance to the child's healthy development.

It is important to identify the presence of traumas as soon as possible, as early treatment can be effective and prevent serious consequences. While the small child can, in its immaturity (and underdeveloped mental structure) be extremely vulnerable, by reason of this same immaturity it has a good chance of reacting positively to a course of infant therapy. However, the longer the time that passes before therapy, the greater the effort required to achieve results.

Traumas experienced during the first three years of life may result in lasting mental and sensory dysfunction.

In the autumn of 2002, Israeli researchers published the results of research involving 50 youngsters then between 14 and 16 years of age born with very low birth weights, and a matching control group of adolescents born at full term (Lubetzky & Gilat, 2002). The youngsters were asked, among other things, to indicate how much they feared personal death, and to answer yes or no to a series of questions relating to social or sensory relationships—an indicator of their ability to handle a crisis.

The research results indicate that the prematurely born had a higher-than-average incidence of:

— fear of personal death;
— attachment styles characterized by insecurity;
— difficulties in handling crisis situations.

In situations of problem solving, the youngsters born too early were liable to resort to avoidance or "fearful–ambivalent" problem-solving strategies.

The researchers concluded that the higher occurrence of fear of death among the prematurely born youngsters had followed upon their hazardous start in life and the higher incidence of insecure attachment styles was partly related to the children's unfulfilled needs and partly caused by the lack of close contact caused by the early mother–child separation.

However, recent research (Zlotnik, 2001) indicates that certain factors—such as female gender, maturity, good, secure family relationships, as well as good social relationships—reduce the risk of health-related influence after traumas. The same factors, together with a low level of stress, contribute in the easing and curing of children's chronic diseases such as asthma.

So, to summarize: traumas suffered by a prematurely born child may cause both mental and physical health problems, but an early concerted effort and the right environment surrounding the child can remedy these.

The immature organs

The organs are immature in the preterm child, and this may cause several problems, particularly during the neo-natal period, but also later on. Lungs, liver, kidneys, and the gastrointestinal system are not ready to carry out their functions when the child is born prematurely. The intensive treatment after birth increases demands on the organs and is, in many cases, a contributory cause of longer-lasting problems.

The structure of the arteries in the very prematurely born child is insufficiently developed, which increases the risk of burst vessel walls. This can contribute to blood pooling in, for example, the brain (Hansen, 1988).

Almost 90% of all newborn children experience a greater or lesser degree of damage or imbalance in connection with the birth (Rosenberg, 2002a, p. 90). The 10th cranial nerve in the neck region may be trapped during the actual birth process or when the child is handled outside the womb—a factor that is often overlooked. When this cranial nerve is trapped, it blocks the flow of the cerebrospinal fluid. This can mean that the nervous system cannot coordinate optimally with the organs. The 10th cranial nerve is a motor, sensor, and parasympathetic nerve, which is connected by nerve endings to almost all the organs, and it is influenced by stress. Among other causes, this may be the reason that the child is plagued with an imbalance of the respective organs.

Additionally, a misalignment or dislocation of the cranial bones (Rosenberg, 2002a), perhaps caused by physical or mental shock, can produce an asymmetrical pressure in the brain hemispheres. This may inhibit development of the brain, and it can be the cause of colic, headache, tension, and stress.

The musculature around the neck vertebrae is not fully developed, which means that the child lacks support from both this as well as from the protective amniotic fluid.

The lungs

The lungs' immaturity means that the child cannot inflate the lungs by itself. The CPAP system is always used as a first priority in Denmark. The respirator, which is less protective of the lungs, is only used if it is absolutely essential.

Apart from this mechanical assistance to breathing, the child is also given medical assistance by, for example, treatment directly in the child's lungs with a surfactant—a substance that lowers the surface tension within the tiny air sacks in the lung, increasing their ability to expand. If the birth does not take place in an acute situation, the child is given a lung maturing medicine by means of an injection given to the mother.

If the lungs and nervous system are not functioning in an optimal manner, the newborn may "forget" to breathe. For this reason the infant is connected to an apnoea apparatus, which sounds an alarm if the child has not breathed for 18–20 seconds. As a rule, it is sufficient to touch the child gently in order to start the breathing again. However, now and then it can sometimes be a little more serious and result in a too slow a heartbeat (*brachycardia*).

Extremely premature babies have a weakened immune system for the first few years, which means that they are more receptive to infections. The immature lungs, which have required treatment for an extended period, may result in the child having problems with chronically occurring complications resulting from such infections. Asthmatic bronchitis, chronic middle-ear infection, and chronic pneumonia are common ailments of prematurely born children before they go to school.

Small premature children have little resistance to respiratory syncytial virus (RS virus). If they become infected while they are still only a few months old, this may mean that they will need help with CPAP-assisted breathing; once the child is a little older, it will generally be able to resist RS-virus infections without breathing assistance. The RS virus, which flourishes from October to March, is characterized by a sticky secretion from nose and throat and violent coughing fits. Penicillin has no effect on viruses—rather, it encumbers the body's immune defences and gut flora and can, in the worst cases, extend and aggravate the course of illness. However, it should be noted, that penicillin might be necessary to treat serious infections that are not of viral origin. The immune defences can be strengthened, and infections can be remedied by means of nutritional supplements. With every passing year, the child copes better with this virus.

The gastrointestinal system

The gastrointestinal system is also immature at birth. The movement of amniotic fluid into the embryo's digestive tract is a necessary condition for the development of the digestive system, as the fluid contains certain growth factors that stimulate the digestive tract into growth. This occurs when the embryo makes swallowing movements and thus swallows the amniotic fluid. Once they are born, premature children must do without this helping hand supplied by nature.

The premature child has a reduced ability to absorb food and may have a weak muscular layer surrounding the closing musculature (gastric cardia), which increases the tendency to gulping and/or vomiting (reflux) (Ibsen, Talbro, & Aastrup, 2000). Such an underdeveloped digestive tract can, for example, be a contributory factor to the difficulty the child has in retaining food, and it can lead to digestive problems. These symptoms are treated medicinally and, in rare cases, by surgical intervention.

The gastrointestinal system's immaturity may be a contributory factor to eating problems later in the infantile period. The child may have difficulties in ingesting sufficient amounts of food at mealtime, partly due to immaturity and the relatively small stomach, and partly due to lacking sufficient strength to eat. The child may also experience pain in connection with digestion, and even a few drops of iron tonic can cause constipation and consequent intense pain.

Wind in the intestinal system is a frequent cause of pain. If the child has difficulty in getting rid of the wind, the resulting outcome can be that the child is hungry but cannot eat because the wind is exerting pressure and causing a blockage. This is a situation that closely mimics the condition called colic.

If the premature infant is not exclusively breastfed, it may experience a lack of lactic acid bacteria in the gastrointestinal system. These bacteria are essential for the proper function of the intestinal tract. The latter exerts an influence on the function of the body's other organs. Lactic acid bacteria can be obtained as a fermented (lactic acid fermentation) mixture of herbs, which can be smeared on the nipple. The child can, in any event, get some lactic acid bacteria just by sucking on the skin. This is why it is a good idea—as well as contributing to the early contact and bonding process—to place the child at the breast as early as possible, even if the suckling and swallowing functions are not yet developed. (This development takes place at about Week 33–34).

The liver

The immaturity of the liver can, in the neonatal period, result in a reduced ability to convert and excrete bilirubin. This factor is generally the cause of jaundice (*icterus*), which is manifested in a more-or-less yellow skin colour. The degree of colouration is dependent on the amount of bilirubin deposited in the skin. The jaundice is treated by phototherapy (light treatment). Supplementary medicinal treatment can be necessary in severe cases.

Jaundice does also carry a risk of deposition of gallbladder pigment in those parts of the brain that influence the coordination of physical movements. If this happens, the child will experience an imbalance in blood sugar; this creates a risk of cramp, and the metabolic fluid and salt balance are disturbed (Hansen, 1988).

The immature liver reduces the child's ability to produce coagulation factors (to prevent congealing of the blood), increasing the child's chances of haemorrhage. Bleeding may occur in the skin, in the lungs, or in the brain (Ibsen, Talbro, & Aastrup, 2000). Briefly, the immature liver may be a contributory factor to an eventual cranial haemorrhage, which can have consequences in the long term.

Therefore vitamin K supplement is given to the child immediately after birth to increase the blood's ability to coagulate.

The kidneys

By Week 36 of pregnancy, kidney development is complete. This means that the ability to concentrate the urine and to convert medication in the kidneys and in the liver is reduced in premature children.

Disturbance of the fluid equilibrium is a frequently occurring phenomenon in newborn premature children. This can occur both as over-hydration and as dehydration. Either can cause a long series of imbalances in all organs. The balance of fluids is therefore kept under close observation during the neonatal period.

If the kidneys do not function optimally, it can reasonably be assumed that this may also have an impact on the child's other organs and its immune defences later on.

Many premature children have difficulties in developing bladder control and may be bed-wetters right up to school age and perhaps even longer. Cranio-sacral therapy has helped many premature children with this problem.

The nervous system and the brain

The nervous system is very immature at premature birth and experiences difficult developmental conditions outside the womb.

The nervous system consists of nerve cells (cell bodies and cell fibres that can send, receive, and act upon impulses). It consists of the brain, the spinal cord, the autonomous system, and the peripheral nervous system (consisting of sensory nerves and motor nerves).

The peripheral nervous system controls all higher nerve functions of importance for movement and senses. By means of the nerve fibres, it receive sensory impressions, whereas the motor system responds to the outward reactions by means of the spinal cord.

The nervous system and the hormonal system control, among other things, the interaction between the organs. This can mean that, for the premature child, the immature nervous system imposes even more difficult working conditions on the immature organs.

The underdeveloped and immature nerve paths take a longer time to transfer impulses.

The limbic system is located in the central area of the brain, close to the brain stem. It is independent of conscious control and represents memories, motivation, recall by mean of smell, the level of stress in the internal organs (or the ability to maintain control and balance in emotionally loaded situations), as well as part of deep emotional life.

The brain's development during the embryonic period

The brain and the central nervous system are very vulnerable during the embryonic development period. In the case of prematurely born children, this development has been abruptly interrupted and has to cope with a life outside the womb. The brain's development, therefore, is central in premature children's risk of latent consequences. The intensive development of the brain's structural shape continues during the first months after premature birth. If the brain is exposed to overstimulation during this period, the risk of greater or smaller neurological damage is increased, affecting the child's behaviour and cognitive development.

Foetal brain development may be negatively influenced if the expectant mother experiences stress during the second and third trimesters (Obel, 2003).

The following description of the development of the embryo is partly inspired by Susanne Freltofte (Freltofte & Petersen, 2001), Tóra Tóroddsdóttir (2001), and Peter W. Nathanielsz (1996).

- *From the 2nd to the 10th embryonic week* the foundation of brain and spinal cord is established.

- *From the 10th to the 20th embryonic week* ca. 200,000 new brain cells are created every minute. They organize themselves into a network, and already by the 10th to 11th embryonic week the embryo is able to "educate" the network of brain cells that will later control walking and suckling reflexes.

- *From the 20th embryonic week to the birth,* the brain cells locate their position, and nerve fibres begin to grow from them.

Some nerve fibres transport signals out to all parts of the body. Others receive signals from the sensing receptors in the skin, eyes, taste buds, ears, and so on.

As this development is thought to continue right up to Week 40, premature children lack a much of this development at birth, and here we find one of the reasons for late motor development and problems with integration of the senses in some of these children.

The child cannot transmit and receive signals in the same way as a full-term child because the brain cells have not yet found their proper place, and all the nerve fibres are not yet grown.

Training and refinement of the pattern of movement begin during the 20th embryonic week, and the nerve fibres begin to work together in a network. Womb contraction during the pregnancy is an important source of input into the embryo's nervous system. The embryo experiences pressure, the oxygen level in the embryonic blood is lessened, and pressure in the head is increased. This stimulates the formation of connections between the nerve cells in the brain. If the child is born several months before term, it must do without this stimulation to development from the function of the womb.

• *From Week 21* the nerve fibres take up so much room that the brain begins to assume its characteristic folds.

In order for the nerve fibres to be used, they have to be isolated from each other. Therefore a layer of fatty substance is deposited around each fibre, and it is this fatty substance that takes up the largest space in the brain.

Only those nerve fibres that deal with the life-essential areas are covered during the embryonic stage, in order to ensure that the head will not become too large for the child to be born.

After birth (at term), nature's coding ensures that the nerve fibres gain fatty deposits in the sequence required by the child in order to acquire new abilities.

• *Only from Week 22* are the reflexes that deal with hearing, sight, and pain reactions trained.

• *After Week 23* the formation of new brain cells declines drastically.

• *From Week 25* the child can survive outside the womb. At this time the child is lacking a great deal of the fatty deposits around the nerve fibres (which represent some 80% of the brain's size), and the unprotected nerve fibres in the brain are not yet in use. A child with a birth weight of 1,000 g contains 860 g water and *no* fat. The rest consists of muscles and organs. A full-term child's body contains 500 g of fat at birth. The premature child must have extra calories in order to manufacture the fatty deposits around the brain, and nature takes care of this: 100 ml premature breast milk contains 80 kcal, while an equivalent amount of normal breast milk contains 60 kcal.

A premature child must also be given protein, in order to support brain development, among other reasons. Experiments have shown that both too little and too much protein can have an adverse effect on intelligence. Boys need more protein than do girls.

This shows the importance of correctly combined nutrition in the infantile period. Thus, when paediatricians judge the combination of the feed, it is not just a question of physical growth but, to an equally high degree, also brain development. If the mother cannot produce sufficient milk for the child, this is often replaced with donated milk expressed from other mothers of premature children who donate their milk to human milk banks (bank milk). The selection process regarding this banked milk is so arranged that premature babies are given milk with an extra high content of protein.

• *From the 26th embryonic week* the nerve fibre network linked to some of the child's reflexes is re-organized and its development is completed. The inborn trained reflexes are the foundation of the child's further motor development—which again acts as the basis for all further learning.

• *During Weeks 28–32* mutually coordinating behavioural conditions begin to appear. The brain now seriously begins to coordinate information received from the senses. At birth children born extremely and very much too early are not able to coordinate the information received via the senses, and, as both the brain and the sensory system have poorer developmental conditions outside the womb, the coordination of the sensory input can become a chronic problem for the premature child, but it can be remedied (see later sections)

The integration of sensory impressions happens thus:

The sensory impressions are received by the child via the sense organs and sent on to the brain, which analyses and harmonizes all impressions into a collected whole. Next, a process of evaluation and selection takes place, to decide upon reaction/behaviour, and the brain sends the relevant message to those nerves that affect muscles and glands.

In very prematurely born children, the brain stem's net structure (*formatio reticularis*), which filters all the sensory input apart from those related to smell, is like the other parts of the undeveloped brain. With this background, along with a poor connection between right and left brain hemispheres, the brain's insufficient chances for development during the child's first months can result in problems with sorting or filtering. The child is thus unable to harmonize the varied sensory impressions into a meaningful whole. It will not be able to differentiate details from the whole and is not able to emphasize a specific impression while pushing others into the background and toning them down. All sense impressions are passed without being filtered and are given equal significance.

• *The final weeks, until Week 40.* The senses are integrated in the part of the brain that develops next to last: the tertiary area at the back of the cerebrum.

Movement is controlled from the front part of the cerebrum, which is one of the last steps in the brain's development.

The cerebral cortex is the final and most highly developed part of the brain. It consists of one quarter of the ca. 100 billion brain cells (neurons) and enables the child to carry out the most complex functions: rational thinking, association of ideas, analysis, and processing of sensory impressions.

When brain development is finally complete, the two hemispheres are connected via a mass of nerve fibres, the *corpus callosum.*

These last-named functions are understimulated and often negatively influenced in the neonatal period if the infant's nervous system is immature and it is exposed to pain, stress, and insufficient positive stimulation of the senses. This may cause the child difficulties during its childhood.

• *Only from the 37th week onward* can the brain control the stages of sleep known as REM/non-REM—that is, light and deep sleep. This means that *all* prematurely born children are unable to control the stages of sleep at birth.

• *By Week 40* the formation of new brain cells stops completely. By this time the brain contains more than 100,000,000,000 (100 billion) cells. The formation of connections between the brain cells continues throughout most of life.

Development of the brain and the senses
outside the womb

Outside the womb the brain, as well the senses, experience difficult developmental conditions. The extreme immaturity of the central nervous system results in breathing difficulties, low motor activity, and reduced muscle tone.

The child has a reduced ability to regulate its blood pressure, and the brain is particularly sensitive towards changes in the blood circulation during Weeks 20–36. Response to treatment-related stress may cause precisely these changes; it can lead to greater or smaller haemorrhages in the brain, as at this time the child also has a reduced amount of prothrombin in the blood (Hansen, 1988). Bleeding within the cranium occurs in 75% of children with a birth weight of less than 1,000 g.

After the 36th week it is usually the cerebral cortex that suffers lesions due to changes in the blood circulation or to lack of oxygen (Trillingsgaard, Dalby, & Østergaard, 2003).

Smaller haemorrhages are not always measurable, and for this reason minor brain damage often goes unnoticed during the neo-natal period. It must be emphasized that we are talking about *minor* brain damage, which may be manifested in, for example, slight paralysis in the legs. This can usually be remedied by training.

Several studies have shown evidence of brain bleeding in 40–60% of all newborn children with a birth weight 1,500 g; however, the more gentle nursing and treatment practised today are the prime reasons why the number of haemorrhage cases has been reduced to ca. 20–25% in this group of children (Peitersen & Arrøe, 1991).

Measurement of brain activity has shown that the brain does not develop while the infant is very ill or in a respirator and concentrates its energy on restoring its physical condition (Brazelton, 1992).

During the first two to three years of life 80–100 million nerve cells are eliminated. This also occurs in full-term infants. But it is important to mention that an overproduction of brain cells takes place during the embryonic development period, and as a result damage caused during the neo-natal period can, in some cases, be "repaired". Other cells take over in areas where an imbalance has arisen. This makes it more difficult to predict the level of functionality in premature children who are afflicted by cranial bleeding.

The brain's physiological structure can be altered by brain damage in connection with birth and events after birth, and also by physical and emotional experiences. Newer research into the brain has shown that it is constantly altering itself in response to psychological influences and that almost all usage and influence of the brain will cause change (Mogensen, 2002). This means that healthy self-esteem, positive self-confidence, a well-functioning social life, a high quality of life, and psychotherapeutic methods can alter the brain in a positive manner.

• *The sensory apparatus,* which is controlled by the body's "computer", the central nervous system, is similarly immature and must cope with unfavourable conditions for stimulation and development outside the womb.

• *The sense of touch (the tactile sense)* is developed in the embryonic state by the constant pressure of the amniotic fluid. Once outside the womb, nothing—duvet, sleeping bag, nor bubble wrap—can act as a substitute for this pressure, and the positive stimulation of the tactile senses is thus impaired. The painful treatment stimulates the tactile senses in a negative manner.

• *The sense of balance (the vestibular sense)* is stimulated by the mother's movements during the foetal development. Long-term bed rest during the pregnancy is a hindrance to the development of the child's sense of balance. A hammock, suspended from a fulcrum, so that the pregnant woman can swing in every direction, will provide a good foundation for the development of balance if long-term confinement to bed is necessary.

The pregnant woman's movement stimulates the child to move. The child is in a weightless condition in the womb and can therefore practise its sense of balance.

Once outside the womb, the infant generally lies supine in a cot and is prevented from practising and developing its balancing abilities.

Research done in Sweden has shown that children in an incubator who sleep on waterbeds or in hammocks develop better.

• *Muscles and joints (the kinetic sense)*: In the final part of a full-term pregnancy, when there is less and less room in the womb, the foetus has the possibility to train and stimulate joints and muscles. The growing foetus can stretch and press arms and legs and push against the wall of the uterus.

In the incubator outside the womb, there is nothing to press the limbs against, and the muscles and joints are not stimulated and developed.

Apart from these three basic sensory areas, the child assimilates sense impressions through light, sound, and smell. The corresponding sensory organs become overstimulated during the course of treatment to the hypersensitive prematurely born child. For many years the child will often be influenced by bright light, loud sounds, and strong smells—particularly smells that have an association with those experienced during the stay in the NICU.

This means that prematurely born children's senses are both over- and understimulated during the treatment period. Without proper and relevant stimulation of the senses, the central nervous system has difficulties in developing as it should. This can lead to altered behaviour. Behaviour can be defined as the end result of the analysis of the collective sensory impressions, which enables us to react to our surroundings (Nathanielsz, 1996). This means that a child whose senses are overstimulated will experience difficult conditions for further development of the central nervous system, and it will react to this.

Other influences

Memory

The memory consists of three memory systems (Fredens, 1998):

personal memory (episodic memory, experiences);
declarative memory (semantic memory, factual knowledge);
procedural memory (memory of procedures, skills).

• *The personal memory* can be divided into short-term memory and long-term memory. What the senses register in the short-term memory can be used, for example, when discussing a text that has just been read and may be forgotten shortly afterwards. The context and message of the text may be moved into the long-term memory if it has made a special impression, if there has been time, peace, and quiet to permit reflection upon what has been read, if the text has been read several times, or if it has been analysed and evaluated—for example, in order to present it to others. One has only learned something when the message and contents of the text is stored in the long-term memory.

Personal memory is linked to time, place, mood, and feelings. It is sometimes referred to as sensory memory. As a rule we are not aware of the personal memory; it is implicit (unconscious).

• *Declarative memory* stores general learned skills like vocabulary, learned systems, numbers, and so on. These skills, or this knowledge, are not dependent upon personal experience, it lies latent in the memory and can be quickly accessed. A personal memory can become a knowledge memory. Once one has personally had the same experience a few times, one can generalize it and make it a habituated routine. The memory is thus not just a store of knowledge: it is a centre of a perception of reality based upon earlier experiences.

• *The procedural memory* holds practical skills such walking, cycling, drawing, writing and playing ball.

Knowledge and those skills that are stored in the long-term memory are the results of a learning process that is either conscious or unconscious.

When one has to draw connections and take the whole picture into consideration, this happens through the unconscious learning process—the personal memory—and this is principally related to the short-term memory.

Parents, teachers, and day-carers often tell of premature children having problems with short- and/or long-term memory. Memory is one of the cognitive functions that frequently are under-developed in very premature children (Stjernqvist, 1999).

A child's sense integration problems may negatively influence the short-term memory because it can be difficult for the child to register impressions in the short-term memory if things are chaotic and disconnected. The child may find it difficult to carry out instructions: it simply forgets the instruction before the task is completed.

If the child is suffering from difficulty in concentration because of stress and unrest, it will find it difficult to store experiences in the long-term memory, because this process requires concentration and the ability to concentrate.

The sense of smell travels directly from the nose into the brain's limbic system without connection to the other senses. This means that when the same smell is present, the child can remember or recall earlier experiences. For example, a visit to the hospital, the smell of disinfectant, or a certain medicine may subconsciously remind the child of the period spent in the NICU, and this can cause an instant reaction, which may be totally incomprehensible at the present time.

Intelligence

Even within an area such as research into intelligence, which, after the development of the IQ test, was characterized by great enthusiasm, there is a decrease as the limitations of these tests become more and more evident. To even be able to investigate questions such as, for example, intelligence, the researchers in these situations are often required to trust the traditional evaluation methods or questionnaires, even though these techniques must be both antiquated and primitive.

H. Rudolph Schaffer (1990, p. 27)

Many investigations and research projects have shown that premature children show a tendency towards lower intelligence. But all these investigations are based on the old IQ (Intelligence Quotient) concept, which is based upon an ability to think in abstract terms, logically, analytically, or mathematically—that is, the ability to learn quickly and precisely.

The perception and the concept of intellect is now broadened by Howard Gardner's (1987) and Daniel Goleman's (1995) theories about many forms of intelligence—for example, sensory, musical, corporeal, language, logical, mathematical, and social. These theories and practical pedagogical models are being applied more and more. Using these newest theories as a starting point, one can question many of the IQ-test results. Based on these newer theories, one can place question marks against many of the earlier results based on IQ tests.

When premature children begin school, any latent problems with concentration and learning difficulties become apparent. If one evaluates the children's presentations, the results are poorer that those of full-term children. In many cases the press has interpreted these research results in terms such as "small children are stupid". This is unfortunate, both because the research into these cases is simply based on the traditional interpretation of intelligence, and also because the results may just as well express the effects of other imbalances or dysfunctions. The child may, due to problems in integrating sense inputs, have difficulties with concentration and understanding tasks, be slow in developing language skills, and/or have a weakened memory and lack self-confidence. A prematurely born child will often feel very insecure in a test situation, where, seated opposite a stranger, it is faced with a need to perform.

One may reasonably ask whether premature children have any chances at all of developing the expected skills if they have a reduced functional level, as described above? May they, as a group, not have a lower-than-average IQ, but simply be slower in reaching the level of expertise expected and be in need of support to this end?

It often happens that premature children with some of these difficulties develop strong skills in those areas where they have strong abilities. This is exactly comparable with physically handicapped children who develop competencies in other areas. And, of course, the children can be intelligent in areas other than those focused upon in IQ tests (in relation to Gardner's and Goleman's theories about many kinds of intelligences). After all, Newton, Kepler, Voltaire, and Churchill were all born much too early.

Dysmaturity (small for date)

Dysmature children—that is, children born with a low weight in relation to their week of birth—have lacked nourishment during all of, or part of, the embryonic period. Insufficient nourishment is a stress factor, and even though early stress is a psychological burden, in this instance there are also positive aspects to the stress.

If the embryo is stressed, the lungs develop better. That means that a premature child born with a lower-than-expected weight will often have fewer respiratory problems than a child born in same pregnancy week, but with the expected weight.

Dysmature children are little fighters. In order to survive a foetal condition of insufficient nourishment and oxygen, they have developed their fighting instincts by producing increased amounts of cortisol and other hormones. By mobilizing all their reserves, they have reacted purposefully and effectively to their stress-filled circumstances.

If a dysmature child is growth-retarded symmetrically—that is, short, with a low weight and with a small head circumference—then the growth retardation *cannot* be caught up.

On the other hand, the dysmature child who is growth-retarded asymmetrically—that is, of low weight, normal length, and normal head circumference—will be able to catch up with growth.

The reason for retarded growth during the embryonic period is generally due to a reduced function of the placenta. This may give an increased chance of developing too-low blood sugar, reduced calcium in the blood (serum calcium), lack of air (asphyxia), and minor motor or intellectual disturbances (Ibsen, Talbro, & Aastrup, 2000).

Causes of pre-term birth

The increasing number of prematurely born children is a general tendency throughout the Western world. The most recent set of statistics from the Danish National Board of Health, for example, shows that in Denmark the number of prematurely born children has increased significantly during the last 20 years: from 4.2% in

1981 to 7.1% in 2001, which equates to about 4,000 children a year. There are, in particular, more children who are born extremely early—that is, before the end of Week 28. In 1981 the extremely early born represented 0.1%, this had risen to 0.3% by 2001—that is, a trebling in 20 years (statistics from the Danish National Board of Health, 2003).

At the same time these years show an explosive increase in the number of children receiving special education. Many of the children are prematurely born (Stjernqvist, 1999).

Several factors account for the increasing number of prematurely born children. The primary cause is the increase in the number of cases of infertility treatment offered to involuntarily childless couples. The treatment results in more twins and triplet pregnancies, and multiple-birth pregnancies carry a significantly increased risk of premature birth. Single-child birth following infertility treatment is also often before term. Today more and more couples are offered infertility treatment in an effort to have a second child, and this will in all probability further increase the number of premature births in the future.

One of the factors that also plays a role is that the treatment of prematurely born children has become significantly better with the passing years, which means that children who would earlier have been registered as still-born are now treated and survive and are therefore included in the live birth statistics.

Reasons for premature birth can be many and very often doctors are too uncertain of the causes to be able to comment on the individual cases. It is known that the pregnant woman's life style can influence the time of birth. Factors such as unhealthy food, smoking, stress, as well as too much alcohol may be contributory factors of too-early birth.

There may also be medicinal and physical reasons, as shown by the following list, collated from a broad investigation of the literature in the area of birth (obstetrics):

— women who were themselves small at birth;

— toxaemia of pregnancy (preeclampsia);

— the water break prematurely;

— bleeding from the placenta (loosening);

— too much amniotic fluid stretches and expands the uterus—
this may, for example, be case in multiple pregnancies;

— the child is not thriving— for example, growth-retarded or
deformed (induction of birth);

— the neck of the womb opens or shortens;

— abnormal conditions in the uterus—for example, increasing
amount of amniotic fluid, increased irritability, deformities;

— surgical intervention during pregnancy;

— illness in the pregnant woman (inducement of birth);

— infection in the pregnant woman is the cause of too-early
birth in 30% of all cases; there is an increased risk with
women in poor nutritional/general health condition, lack of
blood, increased blood pressure, insufficient pregnancy care,
as well as stress;

— women who have previously given birth too early, or who
have previously had a spontaneous abortion after Week 12,
will in the event of a subsequent pregnancy be in the at-risk
group, and the pregnancy will be kept under increased observation; however, ca. 85% give birth at term after a previous premature birth;

— further, a series of low risk factors, such as fever during the
pregnancy, bleeding after 12th week, pyelitis, bacteria in the
urine, the mother's age <17 or >37 years (increased risk if she
is under 17 and over 37 years old), cigarette smoking (more
than 15 per day), low body weight (less than 50 kg).

There is a greater frequency of prematurity among girls, while there
is a greater occurrence of intra-uterine retarded growth (small for
date) with boys.

CHAPTER TWO

Short- and long-term consequences

Casper is frightened of new things. Actually, he has been instantly terrified by some things. This circumstance has improved a great deal since he had some consultations with a psychiatrist. He is certainly not good at school . . . but he definitely is not all that bad either. . . . The teachers have noticed that he finds it hard to concentrate and that he finds things difficult. He "freaks out" when he has to tackle even small problems. He still has a poor vocabulary and difficulty in linking the right words . . . he functions well with his friends—but he never makes the initial contact with people he is not used to. . . . He is not extrovert; he sees new challenges as something danger-ous rather than as something exciting. He is good at football, but his poor physique and lack of height and brawn is gradually becoming a problem for him. Casper has a will of iron: if there is something he wants to learn or to do then he'll persevere until he masters it. Casper has good empathy with others' feelings.

Rune and Jane, parents of Casper (14 years) born Week 36[1]

B ased on the literature, results of research, and, last but not least, my 10-year-long dialogue with parents of premature children as well as day-carers, nursery teachers, and nurses, a clearly defined picture is presented of the hidden handicaps most frequently found in premature children:

— fear and insecurity;

— hyperactivity/hypersensitivity/passivity/aggression;

— frequent infections;

— low self-esteem and lack of self-confidence;

— problems in interaction;

— difficulty in integration of sensory inputs;

— delayed motor development;

— fear of separation;

— problems with eating;

— language difficulties;

— stress and restlessness;

— sleep problems.

As a rule of thumb it can be said that the earlier the child is born, the greater the risk of problem. But there are, naturally, exceptions, and it does happen that a very premature baby avoids any major problems—and, conversely, that a child born at Weeks 33–36 will show several of the typical hidden handicaps as it develops.

Prematurely born children with hidden handicaps do not represent a defined group. Some children may suffer consequences that will appear early in life and are overcome before, or by, the start of schooling. For others such consequences may only become apparent later, sometimes at school age.

Children born too early are naturally as different individually as are all other children. They are full of temperament, which, for example, will be expressed through levels of activity, the ability to comfort oneself, ability to make physical contact, sensitivity, reaction methods and patterns, and the ability to handle stress and difficult situations.

Children who are able to conquer difficulties are characterized by the following traits (Joseph, 1994):

— They are active solvers of problems.
— They are able to use negative and painful experiences in a positive and constructive manner.
— They are easy to be with and are well liked and openly orientated towards others.
— They are goal-orientated and persistent, and they ascribe meaning and value to life.
— They find alternative adults if they are lacking in support and love.
— They are often girls, and they are often the oldest of siblings.

Common to the very prematurely born children is their immaturity, which can cause difficulties with integration of the senses, motor skills, memory, learning, and so on. Common also is the separation and the intense and lengthy treatment that causes the children early traumatic experiences and consequent mental and emotional difficulties as well as social problems. This common foundation shared by premature children can make it difficult for them to find courage, inner strength, and a healthy self-esteem, as well as to have faith in themselves, and thus they find it hard to handle difficulties.

These children have a need for support to develop the above competences; this requires a broad spectrum and continuing effort, but it is possible to achieve. On the positive side, many parents relate that their premature children have a particularly well-developed empathy. It is reasonable to assume that all the physical and mental pain the children have experienced enables them to have insight into other children's feelings. This, however, is only a single skill in relation to full social competence, which also includes social sensitivity, flexibility, altruism, the ability to cooperate, relationship skills, the ability to communicate in social situations, problem-solving skills, self-control, and self-assertiveness (Helgeland, 2002).

Fortunately, it is possible to remedy the effects and consequences premature birth, and a selection of methods to deal with
each topic is given in the following section. Each section refers to
previous sections on causes as well as, where this is relevant, to
following sections dealing with prevention and treatment.

Anxiety and insecurity

> . . . For example, one cannot talk harshly or even firmly to her. Then
> she breaks down and begins to cry. It has become better as the years
> pass, but even so I have had to tell the teachers at her kindergarten
> that they must not scold her—not even if they consider it reasonable
> to do so. One simply must talk gently to her.
>
> Elisabeth Brinch (in Graumann, 1995, p. 58)

Causes and reactions

The Latin word for fear, *angustiae*, means a narrowing. The adjec-
tive *angustus* mean narrow.

Fear is linked to sensations that induce feelings of paralysis or
the urge to flight, and which is connected with weakness, lack of
influence, and helplessness.

Premature children are often frightened of new people, new
things, and new experiences.

In the nursery school it can be difficult for these children to
come into the play area with so many noisy children, new adults,
and many activities. It can be difficult to begin at, or stay in, an
institution, and starting and attending school can be just as difficult.

Quite a few parents report that for many years their premature
children have a more-or-less panicky fear of their own illness, their
own blood, even small scratches. They may become very frightened of, for example, warning pictures of bad teeth or stories about
drinking too many soft drinks, ticks, or other "dangerous" things.
Dentist and doctor checkups can provoke great fear in the child.

Many families of premature children report the need of very many "habituation" visits at the dentist, filled with tears and fear.

During the neonatal period the child has experienced that there were no adults to protect it against discomfort, pain, and separation. When the child is later exposed to heavy mental loads—like, for example, having to change institution or school—this revives the early abandonment and fear: "This is too difficult, and there are no adults who can protect me from this and help me." There may be differing reactions to this, but one of the typical ones is *encopresis* (Lenchler-Hüberts, 2002), which is expressed by involuntary bowel evacuation on the floor or in the underpants.

It is a very heavy and burdensome feeling for the child when it partly cannot control the situation, partly experiences that the adults seen to be of importance do not understand its fear and powerlessness and therefore do not help and protect.

The fundamental fear and insecurity that many premature children exhibit must be ascribed to the early separation from the parents, the unpleasant and even painful care and treatment, as well as the stressing environment on the neonatal ward.

Low self-esteem and lack of trust in others, which is often a consequence of the abovementioned emotional bad experiences in infancy, also contribute to the fear and insecurity in very prematurely born children. Furthermore, the child's reduced ability to function may have a very negative impact on its self-confidence, and this can result in somewhat reserved, reticent behaviour.

Therefore it is extremely important to adjust demands on the child very precisely. Too high a demand will result in the child feeling trapped and having a great fear of being unable to perform, to have to present something. If forced to try to comply with a demand that is too difficult, the child will attempt the task without believing that it can succeed—and so very often it cannot. The child will have a negative experience and a feeling of being "not good enough", which further knocks its self-confidence. So fear can have a disproportionately large importance for the child's ability to develop and to learn.

The fear is deep-seated in the unconscious and may therefore also be expressed during sleep, in the shape of nightmares, problems with going to sleep, and insecurity at sleeping alone.

With premature children there can be fear and anxiety based on the traumas experienced earlier. But the anxiety may also be based on the child's lack of trust of the persons who are caring for it, if they display extreme behaviour such as crude over-protection or total indifference. It is obvious that the one can strengthen the other.

An overprotective style of upbringing keeps the child in a reticent, helpless, narrow world. Conversely, lack of physical contact, lack of stability, indifference, and emotional emptiness will also bring on a state of anxiety.

The child very clearly perceives the parents' feelings and emotional states. If the parents are frightened and fearful on behalf of the child, then this will increase and strengthen the child's own fear. On the other hand, the parents' stability, peace, overview, responsibility, and optimism will tone down the child's anxiety.

Prevention and remedies

After the birth, as soon as the child's condition is fairly stable, the kangaroo method can, and ought to be used. When the child is close to the mother or father's bare skin, it feels secure and protected. The more secure the child feels during this phase, the less anxiety-provoking any unpleasant experiences will be.

The child has a need for Mum and/or Dad to be near 24 hours a day, as is absolutely natural at a birth at term. For a parent it can be difficult to decide whether one should be close to the child, holding it when it has to undergo painful examinations or treatments. One may fear that the child will come to associate the parent's contact with pain. But the parent's care and close presence in these situations will, without doubt, help the child to deal better with the pain, and the child will not feel abandoned in a difficult situation. It is very important that both before and during the treatment the parents speak soothingly to the child, explaining what it about to happen and that it is necessary. One would intuitively do exactly the same when the child is a bit older and has to be given an injection or go to the dentist. The small infant understands voice intonation and body language.

When the child comes home from hospital, it needs firm boundaries, routines, rituals, structures, predictability, preparation of new things, new experiences and changes, small groups, care regarding new experiences or people, closeness, and solicitude.

It is important that the child has faith in and trusts the adult carer and that it feels understood and "seen". A child who has experienced a sensation of betrayal so early in life must have a totally trusting relationship with its parents and feel 100% accepted in order for it to have confidence in itself. In an institution it ought to have a primary person to relate to, and in nursery care it will often be optimal if the child has a funding statement, allowing the normal adult-to-child ratio to be altered so that the child can receive the required additional support.

As deviation, broken routines, new things, and new experiences frequently provoke anxiety or fear in a prematurely born child, continuity and predictability are central concepts when attempting to ensure that the child has a secure everyday life.

The child must be given tasks that are suited to its abilities, and it may need a little help, partly to give it confidence to start on the task, partly to solve the problem. A new challenge that is conquered increases self-confidence and self-esteem. If the challenge is not conquered, it naturally has the opposite effect, and the child's fear of tackling new tasks is reinforced.

The adults involved with the child must accept responsibility and encompass the child's negative emotions. When the child talks about its fear and anxieties—it can be both imaginary and real fear—it needs truthful answers and explanations, orientated according to the child's age, wishes, and needs.

If the child suffers from *encopresis* (involuntary evacuation of the bowels), it has need of more help and support to get through everyday life: for instance, firm agreements with the adults about those conditions that worry the child. The most important part of this work consists in reaching the child and getting it to open up about its fears and worries, so that one has a concrete starting point for supporting the child in the right areas. It can be of great help to tell the child that it is its tummy and not the child that has a problem. In this way the child does not feel guilty and inadequate, and child and adult are standing together to sort out the problem. It may be necessary to seek additional medical help.

Depending on the child's age, infant therapy, sandplay therapy, or NLP (Neuro-Linguistic Psychology) therapy are good tools to get the early experience traumas sorted out and thus help the child in getting rid of anxiety and worries.

The child is often itself able, through play, to partly work through unpleasant experiences it had lived though earlier. The child has a need to be able to play freely and independently without supervision. The more confidence the adults have in the child's independence, the more independent the child will consider itself to be. Parents of a premature child have to forget now and again their own anxieties and worries in order to give the child free rein to be alone or together with friends outside the familiar home surroundings. The child's process of working through prior experiences via play, and its courage to seek independence, are strengthened when it is given a chance to build play-houses in the fields, in the forest, or in some other place and spend hours together with friends, without adults being present.

However, a child with fundamental fear and insecurity also has a need for a firm, constant, loving style of upbringing. Freedom to play by itself, yes, but with firm rules about how far away and for how long.

A fearful child's possibilities for fighting fear and feeling safe are very dependent upon the patience and the personal resources of, and shown by, those who care for the child.

Parents of a child born much too early do themselves and the child a very great favour by getting their own feelings sorted out— feelings that concern the experiences at the birth and during the period after the birth. The parent's unaccepted fear and worry can be contributory to provoking and/or increasing the child's fears.

Hyperactivity/hypersensitivity/passivity/aggressiveness

Children born very much too early do not all suffer from similar difficulties, but are generally more fragile than others, so that even small difficulties can give big problems now and later on. Therefore it is important to keep an eye on even slight problems with the children. The children's nervous system is not fully developed, so their development is very dependent upon the environment, surroundings, upbringing, and genes. Therefore the parent must be very involved.

Hanne Agerholm (2003, pp. 5–9)

Causes and reactions

Infants born very much too early are hypersensitive. They are easily overstimulated and react by, for instance, turning away their heads, crying, yawning, or breathing faster; they make weak or spastic movements or by other means break off the interaction.

Being very small, they can only handle a few seconds of eye contact, and they are rapidly overstimulated by light, sounds, and touch in the form of stroking, lack of tranquillity, and high levels of activity. New experiences, changes, and strangers can trigger crying. The hypersensitive infant is in continual activity; its behaviour is uncontrolled, and it can be inconsolable.

The hypersensitivity is caused by the child's immaturity at birth and the many painful interventions it has experienced. In some cases it can show as tactile shyness, which makes the child react with maximum force to minimal stimuli (Brummerstedt, 2001).

If slightly older premature children are hyperactive, passive or generally aggressive, it may be caused by their hypersensitivity and their lack of ability to integrate sensory inputs. In this case it is a reaction to overstimulation and their helplessness.

A hypersensitive child experiences noise and disturbances significantly emphasized, and it becomes overstimulated and stressed by the many sensory inputs that other children barely register. Reaction and behaviour may differ, but the cause is the same. Children who respond in an extrovert way are aggressive and eventually hyperactive, whereas more introverted children are passive. It is determined by their personality.

Extraverted children, who are overstimulated because of difficulties with integrating input from the senses and difficulties with concentration, will (as babies) react by crying, later by aggression and possibly also by becoming extremely active, but without structure or goals. They are restless, never settle down, and are incapable of waiting. All their actions are driven by impulse, which means that they act before they think. Aggressive and negative behaviour can, in some cases, be ascribed to low blood sugar.

Some children repeat sentences or sing the same verse many times or bang their head rhythmically against the headboard of the bed. This is a method of excluding the many stimuli that the child cannot contain and handle, and it is a clear sign of overstimulation.

Hyperactivity can also be caused by allergies, and it can be one of the symptoms of ADHD (Attention Deficit Hyperactivity Disorder). A diet containing too much sugar may make the child very active, but it is not in itself a cause of hyperactivity.

Where the introverted children are concerned, a clear sign of overstimulation is that the child withdraws to an inner world and is difficult to make contact with.

The brain's immaturity at birth is also the reason why so many premature children show delayed reactions. They can store the day's sense inputs and apparently manage everything well, but then the reaction comes all at once. And this happens when the child is at home in peaceful and trusted surroundings, often during sleep. In this case the child awakes and is restless and crying. If it happens while the child is awake, it will also be restless and possibly crying or aggressive.

Delayed reactions can mean that day-carers, teachers, relatives, and friends who are typically together with the child while all the sensory inputs are experienced do not witness the consequent reaction. This often creates misunderstanding.

Prevention and remedies

These difficulties can first and foremost be met by low stimulation. This may mean that the child needs to be kept at home for a longer time, and that it should be exposed to a limited number of impressions and experiences. This includes, for instance, the daily period of peace at home where there should be only one sense stimulation at a time. During infancy, when the child is breastfed or given the bottle, it may be overstimulated if other activities are going on during the meal. This can be just eye contact, petting, rocking, humming, or something similar.

The hypersensitive infant, who is often inconsolable, needs, in addition to few stimuli, tranquillity, quiet, and loving care, parents who exude self-confidence in their role as parents. The parents' calm and determination, optimism, and conscious support arrangements can create secure boundaries and help with the organization of the nervous system and thus of the child's self-control (Brazelton, 1992).

Television and music playing as background noise can easily overstimulate the premature child, and this stimulation continues past infancy.

Pastel colours without patterns induce tranquillity and do not overstimulate the visual senses. Green, lilac, pink, and blue act in a calming manner, whereas red, yellow, and orange are stimulating.

A hyperactive child needs help to structure its energy and maintain concentration by means of firm routines and rituals, just as it is important for the child to be given clear, direct requests and clearly defined tasks. If the child is being active without having a specific goal, it can be helpful to ask the child about its plans and projects. This stimulates the child to take stock of its activities, make some decisions, and set some goals, and it gives the adult carer the possibility of helping the child to concentrate and continue its activity.

As hyperactivity, passiveness, and aggression are often reactions against overstimulation due to hypersensitivity and insufficient ability to coordinate the sensory inputs, physiotherapy, and ergo (occupational) therapy can be good treatment forms. Craniosacral therapy can also be recommended. If the child shows delayed reactions at home, one ought to be aware each time what it is that the child has been exposed to during the previous 24 hours and thus try to identify the source of the overstimulation. If sudden, unexplained reactions, the cause of which is not always understandable, create misunderstanding in connection with people, it can be a good idea to hand out literature about the phenomenon and/or explain further.

One ought also to be aware that healthy and nourishing food has significance for the child's mental and physical condition.

Frequent infections

Søren has just celebrated his fifth birthday. It took three days before the nursery school, the grandparents, and the rest of the family had celebrated his day. This proved to be too much for him, so now he is in bed with a fever and cough again. He is still not sufficiently robust to handle so much excitement, which we naturally should have known.

Private letter from Mie Andersen, mother of son born Week 30.

Causes and reactions

The immune system must fight about 250 infections or "attacks" every 24 hours, and is thus constantly at work in all children and adults.

The weakened immune system with which many premature children have to battle during their first 2–3 years of life may be caused by immature airways and overburdened lungs, an immature central nervous system, a lack of growth, possibly a lack of antibodies from the mother's milk, having early and wide-ranging dosages of medication, long exposure to stress, and repeated infections starting in the neonatal period. Both acute and chronic stress can increase the occurrences of infection, diseases, and allergies (Zlotnik, 2001).

These factors mean in many cases that the child is very receptive to infection and that infection can result in chronic disease. The most frequent of these are asthmatic bronchitis, chronic pneumonia, and chronic middle-ear infection. The Danish State Institute of Health has undertaken an investigation (Nielsen, 2002), which shows a clear difference in the occurrence of infection, diseases, and allergies in breastfed children when compared to children fed with milk substitutes: children who had been breastfed for four months did not suffer from middle-ear infections, wheezy breathing, gastrointestinal difficulties, high fever, and other symptoms of illness as often as did bottle-fed babies.

Prevention and remedies

During the initial period mother's milk, suckling at the breast, loving care, and high standards of hygiene will best protect the child against infections. One must be aware that some antibodies contained in mother's milk are totally or partly destroyed by freezing. Expressed breast milk can be kept safely in the refrigerator for up to 72 hours. Later it will often be an advantage if the child is nursed for a longer period at home in order to avoid infection and to strengthen the immune system in safe surroundings, away from many new and varied bacteria.

Other major factors are healthy food, fresh air, no damp, no smoke, as well as a very high standard of hygiene. It is especially important to ensure that all members of the family wash their hands frequently. As far as possible avoid letting the child come into contact with other children or adults who are suffering from a cold, particularly during the autumn and winter months. If the premature child has siblings, it is naturally difficult to avoid infection, but one can make sure that the siblings wash their hands and change their clothes when they return home from public places such as school.

To help clear blocked noses, it is possible to buy naturally produced nose drops and nasal sprays. One can also rinse the nose with saline water, which can be obtained from the pharmacy in little pipette bottles. If chemically produced preparations are used for a long period, the nasal mucous lining becomes irritated, swells up, and secretes mucus, and in this manner the cold symptoms continue, but now caused by medication.

If there is a tendency towards infection, one should be aware that milk products are mucus promoting and can thus worsen the child's condition.

Cranio-sacral therapy, reflexology, and nutrient supplements can help to strengthen the immune system and remedy infections.

Concentration and learning disability

Several large investigations have found that various influences during the embryonic period or during or just after birth are very much more common in children with difficulties with concentration than in other children. Reasons may be that the child was born too early or that it had received too little nourishment from the placenta.

Björn Kadesjö (2002, p. 92)

Causes and reactions

Various investigations have shown that some 50% of all children born with a birth weight of less than 2,500 g suffer from difficulties with concentration, difficulties in learning, and consequent social problems at school (Kruuse, 1984) and that in children born much too early there is an increasing occurrence of developmental deficiencies (Roth, Baudin, Pezzani-Goldsmith, Townsend, & Reynolds, 1994) and of minor neurological malfunction as they get older (Lunsing, Hadders-Algra, Huisjes, & Touwen, 1992, Zubrick, Macartney, & Stanley, 1988). There is a predominance of boys in these groups.

These investigations are based on children of school age where one knows from experience that some premature children who receive good support from the parents and professionals have totally or partly overcome these difficulties.

A child suffers from difficulties with concentration if it has difficulty in focusing its perceptions, thoughts, and feelings on a specific task, if it cannot exclude irrelevant sensory impressions, and if it has difficulties in beginning, continuing with, and completing a task.

Limited ability to concentrate and to learn are often only discovered when the child reaches school age, when there are greater demands in these areas.

But it is possible to uncover eventual difficulties much earlier. As soon as the child is able to sit by itself, one will be able to observe if it is able to play with the same toy for a long period or if it only sits with a toy for a short while and then discards it in favour of a new one—a sign of concentration problems.

Once again we find the cause for this in the immature nervous system and brain, which experienced difficult developmental conditions during the infancy period. The integration of sense impressions and motor-skill development has a great effect on the child's ability to concentrate.

A poor memory can also be a contributory factor in learning difficulties. If the child cannot remember a message given earlier or things previously learned, it will not have the prerequisite foundation for adding new knowledge. Perception may be underdeveloped, and this can be a contributory cause of learning difficulties.

If the child cannot understand, coordinate, and then arrive at a conclusion from its sense input, it will have difficulties in learning, which is, after all, totally dependent on the faculty of cognition. This can manifest itself in an in ability to recognize numbers and letters and to orientate these the right way round.

Noise pollution has a negative influence on certain cognitive processes (Zlotnik, 2001). Furthermore, the immature brain's disturbed development once outside the womb can give the child problems with cognitive functions. This will mean that the child will find it difficult to reason and to find possibilities and solutions based on its knowledge and experiences.

The area of research into stress is very involved with aspects of concentration, memory, and learning, with specific focus on treatment with substances that stimulate the central nervous system—for example, *Ritalin*. There are indications that stress is one of the causes of the great increase in the number of children who require special education (Zlotnik, 2001), out of which number the prematurely born represent a significant part (Stjernqvist, 1999).

Learning difficulties can occur in several areas, and it is worth while to be aware of the many types of intelligence through which to recognize and support the child's resources and strong aspects.

Concentration difficulties, as well as learning difficulties in the areas of mathematics, reading, and spelling can also be related to the visual sense. This develops step by step through the maturing process and is very dependent upon motor-skills development. All the child's developmental steps are of significance for the development of vision, and it does, occasionally, happen that the child skips some developmental stages or that other disturbances hinder the development of visual skills.

Trauma, too much reading, too much screen-work, many middle-ear infections, premature birth and/or birth by Caesarean section may also prove to be a link with eventual later visual problems. Foods that contains too little fibre and/or too few vitamins, minerals, and polyunsaturated fatty acids as well too many empty calories can also contribute to difficulties with concentration and learning.

Difficulties in learning must, in the long tern, influence the child's self-confidence. Repeated experiences of defeat in connection with the demands of learning can create a lack of faith in the ability and desire to learn and thus reinforce the difficulties. A child who senses that there is no point in making an effort because it most likely will not give any result loses motivation and finds it even more difficult to concentrate, pay attention, and learn.

Prevention and remedies

Difficulties in maintaining concentration can be toned down by limiting sensory impressions, ensuring tranquillity, taking breaks, and letting the child stay in small groups.

Play provides every possible chance for the development of the child's ability to concentrate, and a high degree of physical expression is also very important. But in order to tackle the root of the problem, it is necessary to use physiotherapy or occupational therapy and/or cranio-sacral therapy, which will, for example, help to establish the incomplete connection between the right and left hemispheres of the brain. Cranio-sacral therapy can also recreate the rhythm of the nervous system and thus remove eventual blockages that burden and reduce the brain's function, including the ability to concentrate, perception, and memory.

Healthy and nourishing food also plays a significant part in the child's concentration and learning ability.

In everyday life one can, for example, strengthen concentration by helping the child to become engrossed in play, in a book, or in other things that capture the child's interest; it is always easier for the child to concentrate upon something it considers interesting, fun, or exciting. One can then slowly increase the time spent, so that the child is stimulated to concentrate upon something for longer periods at a time.

The demands made on the child must be adjusted to its abilities, and it is necessary to be continually aware of when the child is participating and concentrating and when it is acting on impulse and without awareness of strategy or goal. The lack in self-confidence, which is a consequence of the child's difficulties, demands that the child is continually supported in this area. It must have tasks and challenges that it can deal with to its own satisfaction, and this happens best when one can focus the demands to suit the child's areas of competence.

There are a great many books and Internet sources discussing various methods of helping children to concentrate. Readers are recommended to consult these, but to evaluate the literature carefully, especially Internet items where many of the published "recommendations" are thinly disguised sales vehicles for various nutritional supplements.

Two books—one produced by the NSW Multicultural Health Communication Service, *Helping Children with Concentration Problems: A Guide to ADD, the Signs and Where to Get Help* (November 1998) and another by Lee Hausner, *Teaching your Child Concentration: A Playskool Guide* (1998)—also give very good advice on the topic.

An improved ability to concentrate will contribute to better learning, but memory also plays a role. This can be trained by, for example, giving the child responsibility for remembering something specific. One can help by giving the child, or letting the child make, a note with a drawing or message that will assist in memory recall. Together with the child, one can place the note in a place where one knows it will be seen at the time the child has to remember to do something. It can also be beneficial to attach a loved possession to the "remembering" exercise—for example, one can, together with the child, put one of the child's treasures into the games bag in the morning. This considerably increases the motivation to remember to bring the bag back home.

It may often be necessary to operate at several levels with a child who has learning difficulties—for example, to talk with a 10-year-old child at the level usually used with a 12-year-old and to carry out sport and motor training at a level suited to a 6-year-old and mathematics at an 8-year-old level.

A child with learning difficulties in only a single area can be supported by putting a special effort into those areas where the child has its strengths. The child has greater pleasure in developing strong skills in specific areas than achieving average all-round knowledge by hard training and extra teaching, partly because it strengthens self-confidence and gives a feeling of self-esteem if the child can present something extraordinary, partly because it motivates the child to undertake further learning. Supporting (extra) education can be useful when the child has difficulties in following the required syllabus, but it is important to realize that training in reading, for example, will not be able to remedy reading difficulties that are caused by impaired sense functionality. A child with learning problems caused by a lacking or impaired ability to sort out sensory inputs has a need for training in integrating the various inputs sent by the senses in order to become better at reading and/or arithmetic. If learning difficulties are caused by problems with the sense of vision, a specific individual effort can improve the lack in abilities. Reduced vision is not as evident as are problems with motor function, behaviour, hearing, and speech. But by observing and asking the right questions it can be deduced whether the reasons for the learning difficulties are caused by the child's vision.

Training vision does not include training in reading, but the training helps to provide the right tools to optimize the learning process. In this way the child is given the right prerequisites and subsequent desire to learn and will quickly make great progress.

Signs of vision-related learning difficulties (www.syn-udvikling.dk; see also www.add-adhd.org/vision_therapy_FAQ .html):

— slow reading speed;
— text is followed by finger or bookmark;
— the head, not the eyes, follows the text;
— repetition or missing out a line; losing place in text;
— seeing double/shadows around the letters;
— transposing "b" and "d";
— reading short words backwards/transposing words;
— abnormal distance from text;
— missing out words in the text;
— problems with eyes/headache when doing close work;
— lacking concentration;
— the text is "moving";
— difficulties in playing ball games;
— shutting or covering one eye while reading.

At present there are still very few clinics specializing in vision and development.

A healthy self-esteem, no stress, physical exercise, the bones of the cranium in place, and balance of the central nervous system are the key factors for a good ability to learn.

Negative self-esteem and lack of self-confidence

If I consequently need to identify weaknesses related to my too early birth it must be that I am . . . uncertain of my self-esteem and unduly cautious over big challenges away from my home.

Bente Bertelsen (2003, pp. 43–44)

Causes and reactions

Self-esteem or self-awareness concerns what the child is in its inner core, while self-confidence results from what the child can do or does.

Many children born too early have a negative or low self-esteem for many years, and only a very small amount of self-confidence. It is very common to find that a prematurely born child does not have the courage to accept new challenges, large or small. Infants are, as a rule, eager to learn, and parents and teachers are driven to distraction by the cry "I want to do it myself!" and "I can do it myself!"

It may be several years before one has the pleasure of hearing these words from a child born much too early. Here it is more common to hear, "I don't want to, you do it", "I'm scared", and so on. Common small everyday matters, ranging from having the courage to tie one's shoelace, to going to a birthday party, telephoning a nursery or school friend, or learning to ride a bicycle can cause immense problems for the child.

This is a condition and behaviour that is typical of a child who has been exposed to early separation and who has, through this, acquired a feeling of having been betrayed, of not being "good enough". Not only the separation, but also the treatment can have an influence on the child's subsequent perception of itself. A child born very much too early has been in contact with many new and different people who have, from its first day in the world, caused it pain and discomfort, which has given the child the impression that it is not loved. It may also be a case of bad parent–child inter-action caused by the difficult conditions and the child's very weak signals. And finally, the unfulfilled desire for peace, security, and positive stimulation during the neonatal period can have a nega-tive influence on the feeling of self-esteem.

Delayed language development, social problems, as well as behavioural difficulties caused by the inability to coordinate sense impressions and/or correlation problems can cause low self-es-teem and a lack of self-confidence, which can, in turn, result in learning difficulties.

The child can convince itself that it cannot do something, and this then becomes reality: it cannot do it, even though the abilities really are there.

Self-esteem and self-confidence are incredibly important factors for the child's pleasure in life and quality of life.

Prevention and remedies

For the child's feeling of self-value and self-esteem to be strength-ened, it needs close ties, care, trust, total acceptance, and confirma-tion of itself—that is, avoidance of negative criticism.

It is not important "whose fault" it was that something was dropped or that a misunderstanding arose. If the adult refrains from blaming the child and possibly claims responsibility for the mishap, it will contribute to building a stronger feeling of self-esteem.

Who—adult or child—feels of greater worth if told that "You should have thought that out first" or "You should have been more careful!"? The child has a need to know that adults caring for it can encompass and accept heavy negative feelings such as fear, sorrow, and anger. Furthermore, there is a need for adults to accept some responsibility by, for instance, expressing understanding and by helping the child to put the feelings into words.

But even if the child must be "seen", understood, and sup-ported, it must also understand that it has to accept some respon-sibility. The child certainly has a need of support to confront its fears and anxieties, but it does strengthen its feeling of self-esteem if involved in dealing with its own fears and insecurity.

Self-confidence can be given a helping hand by the adults supporting the child in crossing boundaries and thus giving it the chance to experience success. If the child has a tendency to turn away from new challenges as mentioned above, there may be a need for a long and continuing input by the adults who care for the child. The child is best helped if one does not do those things that the child is frightened of attempting, but instead insists that the child should do it, initially with some help from the adult. This "practice" may have to be done many, many times, but it does give very positive results in the long run.

Also praise—to a limited extent—helps to build up self-confidence.

In some situations the demands on the child can be too great, and then it is best to wait until the child is more prepared. It will be a matter of fine judgement as to when the child should have help to cross boundaries and when it has a need for more time and preparedness to take this particular step.

Problems in interacting

To catch a feeling, to grasp a thought
of flowing clarity and spirit,
is like holding a prematurely born
and trembling life in one's hand.

Tove Ditlevsen (1955, p. 5)

Causes and reactions

Interaction problems between parents and child can occur as early as in the neonatal period. The child's signals are weak and can be difficult to interpret.

For instance: is the child tired or overstimulated when it yawns? Is it turning its head away from the breast or bottle because it is satisfied, or because it has problems with wind in the gastrointestinal system?

The immaturity of the nervous system and of the brain at birth are one of the reasons for the child's weak signals.

In the beginning the parents may find it difficult to dare to form an attachment with their child, or they may have difficulties in accepting that it is their child who has need of them and their care.

The early separation of parent and child may result in long-lasting problems regarding interaction. As mentioned in the section "The Child's Experience of a Pre-term Birth", the child's perception of being betrayed can mean that it later feels an unconscious anger towards its mother.

John Bowlby, the major figure behind the attachment theories, has proposed that infants are pre-programmed to develop themselves as socially interactive. How far they do this is to a great extent dependent on the way they are treated. Bowlby says that the perception of security or insecurity during the child's early interaction with the parents influences its later emotional relationships and personality. He has undertaken research that shows that the child has a very poor ability to form intimate relationships with other people if it has totally or partially lacked contact with the mother (Bowlby, 1988). It is an unhappy situation in that parents of infants born extremely early or very early who are therefore ill do not have the possibility of giving the child optimum care and security, even though this is their dearest wish. The parent cannot be the child's secure base during the intensive course of treatment—there is *no* secure base, because no one can protect the child against pain, discomfort, and separation. This means that it will often become extremely difficult to create attachments and positive interaction later on.

The parent's shock at the premature birth and the subsequent crisis or difficulties can mean that they will be lacking in self-control, in the ability to take a broad view, and in reserves of strength. As a rule they are frightened that they will lose their child, and they are frightened that the child may be handicapped and the infant senses their fear, worry, and anxiety. Shock, fear and insecurity in both parties are very unfavourable circumstances under which to begin a parent–child relationship.

Some premature children are unable to breastfeed for various reasons, and this can prove to be a further obstacle to establishing a mother–child relationship. This must not be taken as meaning that a good mother–child relationship can *exclusively* be established if the child is breastfed, but the breastfeeding is of great help in this.

Later in the course of things, eating problems, hyperactivity, sleep problems, fear of separation, repeated infections, and many other things can contribute to the parents being drained of energy and thus finding it very difficult to come out of the vicious cycle of poor interaction.

A lack of close relationship to the parent can increase the child's insecurity, and it can become frightened and withdrawn. But a child who, after about six months of age, experiences many different faces each day and is passed from arm to arm does not learn to differentiate between known and strange persons and will behave in an unsuspecting and uninhibited way in relation to others. This should not be taken as an expression of feeling secure, but as a sign of poor attachment (Rogge, 1998).

In its interactions with other children, the premature child can be a bit reserved and hesitant, a bit insecure and anxious. But it may also find it difficult to understand the rules of the game, which means that it will often react inappropriately to the dissatisfaction of other children. This can be caused by a variety of things, such as hyperactivity, early and/or home integration problems, difficulties with concentration, as well as that the child is at a different developmental level.

The last-mentioned cause means that the child will find it difficult to become involved and immersed in the game, because it cannot follow the rules of the game.

If a child with these problems is not observed and understood in the right way, it may be perceived as having behavioural difficulties, which both children and adults may perceive in a negative manner, and the child can find that it is often excluded from play.

Children with reduced functional abilities are significantly less often in contact with other children, and any contact there is, is of short duration or sporadic (Ottosen & Bengtsson, 2002).

Prevention and remedies

In the case of a very early or extremely early birth there is an extraordinary requirement for the staff on the neonatal ward to help the parent with translating the child's signals. These naturally become clearer and clearer as time passes, so any problems in this area should be temporary.

The closeness, love, and care shown by the parents is invaluable for the child; even though the very tiny infant may not immediately respond with smiles and a happy expression, one must in no way fail to appreciate the value of this for the child.

Once the child is past infancy and is able to express its feelings in ways other than by crying, it may show anger, which can be difficult to understand and find the cause of at the time. If this anger is felt in the child, who is possibly directing it particularly at the mother, then infant therapy or, later, sandplay therapy may prove beneficial. Also, conversations with the child about events and feelings in the period after birth can reveal the cause of the anger. The child needs to realize that the separation was not caused deliberately, but could not be prevented, was related to outside circumstances, and was not intended as betrayal.

The child has a need of the parents' and perhaps professional carers' support in the adjustment process, but it does not need to have all responsibilities taken from it.

The child itself has enormous competence with which to work with negative feelings such as, for example, fear and anger. The child uses play, fantasy, and rituals, which also form some of the ingredients of sandplay therapy.

John Bowlby calls the mother "the secure base" to which the child can return at any time when it is frightened, when it feels threatened or insecure. When the mother is not physically present, the child will, in Bowlby's words, use a security blanket or a "sucking cloth". This can be a soft bedtime toy, blankets, cloth nappy, a thumb, or something else that gives the child security. The child who seeks out these substitute objects is demonstrating its competence at calming itself (Bowlby, 1988).

Even in the incubator it may be of great value for the child to have, for example, a little scarf that smells of Mum.

The infant must have limitless solicitude, satisfaction of its needs, and love. But attachment behaviour that gives an infant stability and security may, for a 3-year-old child, mean that it feels itself suffocated and somehow crushed; such a child will not develop independence and relevant presentation skills. The parents' attachment behaviour and methods of bringing the child up must, in other words, always be adjusted to suit the child's age and state of development.

It will be of benefit to the child if the parents work through and analyse their own experiences in relation to the premature birth. An adult, who is carrying unexplored fear, anger, sorrow, and so on, is unable to optimally take in and comply with the child's equivalent emotions.

If the parents are aware of the causes of the child's fears, they themselves can avoid feeling fear in this connection; this is, in itself, of great support for the child.

Problems caused by difficulties in interacting can, additionally, be helped by massage, care, and close contact. If the child fends off close contact with one or both parents, holding can be a good tool to use. The Marte Meo method (see below) is unique in the identification and solving of problems with interaction.

Interaction with other children

When children are interacting with each other, it is important to give them space so they can get to learn and know each other. This can include common activities organized by adults. An unambiguous and clear instructive direction play a role, as do daily routines that build the child's capabilities for becoming a part of the group. A child with interaction problems often needs help from an adult or another child to assist it in becoming accepted into the "gang" or group. The responsible adult ought to observe the children at play with other children to gain an understanding of the character of the interaction problems, so a foundation for a suitable effort can be formed.

The child may also have a need for an adult to help it to alter its self-perception. If the child has a negative or destructive opinion of itself, this will be expressed in its interaction with other children.

If the child has done something that is inappropriate, it must be helped to understand just what it is that it has done; but this should be done in such a way that the child senses that it is loved despite its actions. If the child has, for example, hit another child, it must be told that it has hurt the other child and that the other child is upset. It must also be told that such behaviour will not be tolerated. If one asks the child about the reason why it hit the other child, one may be able to decipher its pattern of behaviour; this may be the key not only to change this but, through this change, also create a better foundation for improved interaction.

There will also be individual need of support, as in the case of children with speech and language difficulties, reduced vision and/or hearing, delayed motor development, and problems with integration of the senses.

If the difficulties with interaction are totally or partly caused by hyperactivity, then the reason behind this may be underdeveloped areas in the brain and nervous system, which can be remedied by, for example, cranio-sacral therapy, physiotherapy, or occupational therapy.

Sensorimotor training of hyperactive children and of children with difficulties in integrating their sense impressions is important, but will not alone suffice. These children's impulse-driven behaviour additionally demands a special education built primarily on firm rules.

Difficulties with sensory integration

Many children with fundamental difficulties in integrating their sense impressions have a need—as well as for physical stimulation—also a need for psychological help. To have lived with the problem of integrating the sense impressions is physically wearying, and it is possible that the child's self-perception and self-confidence is so damaged that it will need psychological treatment.

Tóra Tóroddsdóttir (2001, p. 78)

Causes and reactions

Where integration of the sense impressions is concerned, once again we find the root cause in the central nervous system and the brain. Sensory integration (SI) is the ability to receive, organize, differentiate, and analyse stimuli from the senses so as to be able to integrate these in the right rhythm and at the relevant level—both inner stimuli from the body and external stimuli through, for example, vision, hearing, smell, taste, touch, with the purpose of action. Stated very briefly—the ability to collate the many impressions into a cohesive whole.

The child who has difficulties in integrating or collecting impressions from all these sources into a meaningful entity becomes overstimulated, and its inner world becomes chaotic. Sense impressions that the child itself has explored, and is thus prepared for, rarely induce overstimulation.

Most infants—some 85% of them—have a period of crying towards the end of the day, where they "let off steam" and reorganize their nervous system. Minor or more serious disturbances of the central nervous system will cause a special shrill, piercing crying, which reflects the infant's hypersensitivity and inner chaos (Brazelton, 1992).

In a slightly older child SI problems will be expressed through the child becoming easily overstimulated, easily frightened, sensitive to noise; such a child may lack stickability, have motor-skill problems and possibly delayed language development, may find it difficult to understand an order given to a group or a sequence of messages, may be insecure and reticent, and have difficulties with making decisions, with concentration, and thus also with learning.

For instance, the child may be unable to pay attention to a conversation if there is background noise in the room, because for the child the background noise will appear just as clear as the words in the conversation.

These SI problems can give the child mental and social difficulties. For the sensitive and vulnerable child it can be very hard to lose self-control and to run around in a hyperactive manner, which can be the outcome of massive overstimulation. It is also difficult for the child always to be the one who cannot do things, who always takes too long about everything, who does not quite understand. This can result in the child becoming more and more reticent in social circumstances and in connection with demands of presentation.

A child who finds it difficult to integrate sense impressions and coordinate motor movements may keep bumping into things and be generally clumsy. Or it may find it difficult to carry out a sequence of goal-orientated activities, like, for example, to do a somersault or to tie a shoelace.

Generally children with SI problems often also have problems with gross motor skills, fine motor skills, and cognition; and if they also have negative attitudes such as fear, stress, low self-esteem, and lack of self-confidence, there are many factors that play a part in the child's condition and behaviour. But if the problems are not too serious, they are often overlooked, because they are not immediately obvious. Quiet and more introverted children, in particular, are often left to cope with their problems alone. Parents can almost always sense when their child's difficulties are caused by dysfunction, including SI problems, and this can create a problem between parent and professionals because the latter rarely have the same deep understanding and perception of the child; this is why it can be extremely difficult to get help with defining and remedying the child's dysfunctions.

Conversely, it can also happen that the SI problems do not affect the child very much at home, because it is a secure place with very few sense impressions and with plenty of time to receive the impressions. In an institution—and particularly at school—greater and different demands are required, which can be difficult for the child to live up to.

Even though they are the result of a brain dysfunction and thus are physically determined, SI problems cannot be diagnosed as such; they are deduced through observation of the child and carrying out tests, and only a trained observer can judge the degree of difficulties (Ayres, 1979).

The child physiotherapist Tóra Tóroddsdóttir (2001) found from experience that it is easy for the trained eye to tell the difference between children who only have SI problems and those who have additional difficulties. A child who has exclusively SI problems has a natural behaviour pattern when the surroundings are suited to its needs. It can work for a long time with focus and concentration if it is given peace and the task is suited to its capabilities. A child who has, in addition, other and greater problems will, despite good progress in dealing with the task, be unmotivated to continue with the task after a short while and will give up. It will have an unstable contact with the adult who is present. It will rapidly become tired when it has to solve problems that others control and define.

A child with SI problems may be suffering from ADHD, which is often accompanied by several other difficulties. This concerns, for instance, behavioural dysfunction, passivity, irregular sleep patterns, motor problems, and speech and/or language difficulties. However, all these symptoms are more or less common in premature children, and for these children the causes of the difficulties are obvious as one is aware of the brain's diminished developmental conditions during the period of early infancy.

The perception of definitions and terminology within the areas of learning and behavioural difficulties, motor problems as well as sensory integration, have been vague and ill defined. Before the ADHD concept became commonly used, the description was MBD (Minimal Brain Dysfunction). Other diagnoses are related to ADHD (from DAMP-Foreningen [The DAMP Society], Denmark):

— hyperkinetic disturbances;

— DAMP (Deficit in Attention, Motor Control, and Perception): a Scandinavian diagnosis, which has a broader spectrum than ADHD;

— ADD (Attention Deficit Disorder): difficulties in concentrating;

— DCD (Developmental Coordination Disorder), which focuses upon difficulties with motor centres, perception, and feelings.

The diagnosis of ADHD is often only made once the child is 5–6 years old, and in some cases even later. The diagnosis is made based on the background of exhaustive investigation and observation and also based on the parents' and educationalist's/teacher's statements.

One can ask oneself whether it is the one or the other—ADHD or "only" the appearance of latent handicaps—but the value of the designation lies in the fact that it can help to define the child's difficulties and indicate the help required.

Prevention and remedies

To prevent and remedy SI problems, it is naturally necessary first to observe and identify them. This can be difficult, as it is somewhat uncertain when one can expect each stage in the premature child's development—particularly if it has suffered with many infections and airway illnesses, and so on. It can become even more difficult if the child has been cared for at home for some years and has not been treated by a physiotherapist or an ergo therapist, because the parents are thus almost sole observers. In this situation the visiting surgery nurse plays an important role, initially as an observer and eventually as initiator of action. The SI problems are thus in many cases only identified once the child attends an institution or school.

Questionnaires aimed at respectively educationalists and teachers are available in several versions. These questionnaires may be of help in identifying the child's difficulties.

The child who has SI problems must not be overstimulated. It needs quiet surroundings, with few people close by. It should not be expected to have to make too many decisions, it needs brief, direct and precise information, and it will need help to structure its day for everything—small and large. It is important that demands and expectations of the child are kept to an attainable level.

It can be of help to the child to be held somewhat tightly by an adult when it is exposed to impressions that are difficult to assimilate. These can be the effects of touching, sound, light, smell, or movement.

A ball blanket or a ball cushion (see below) damp down the impulses sent to the brain and can thus reduce the strength and intensity of sense impressions.

The child does not "grow out" of SI problems. Limiting the sense inputs, stimulating through play, and initiation of educational support are some of the methods that can anticipate the child's special needs. But actual remedy of the difficulties requires treatment—for example, in the shape of physiotherapy or occupational therapy involving SI exercises and/or cranio-sacral therapy.

Physiotherapy or occupational therapy can teach the child skills that may compensate for poor sense assimilation, but they cannot remove the neurological disturbances that are the root cause of the problems. The therapy is prolonged and includes training as well as special attention to the child's needs, environment, and condition. Through therapy the child is given help to organize the nervous system by means of precisely adjusted challenges, which are perceived by the child as play. The therapist, who must have special knowledge about and experience with sensory integration, may be employed by the council, the county, or the local hospital's children's section, or may work in private practice. The surgery nurse or the children's outpatient ward at the hospital should be able to provide information about whom to contact.

Cranio-sacral therapy (see below) can help to change the neurological disturbances by loosening the brain membranes (dura mater, falx cerebri, and tentorium), by which means the spinal fluid in the central nervous system can circulate freely. The therapy can establish connection between the brain hemispheres by just a single treatment. It would, however, be necessary and reassuring to have a follow-up treatment; also other minor dysfunctions may be revealed, and the therapist will need to treat these during further sessions (articles and documentation relating to cranio-sacral therapy can be found at www.upledger.com).

Cranio-sacral therapy may be of greater benefit if it is supplemented with "cross-training", the objective of which is stimulating coordination between the brain hemispheres by means of cross-movement with arms and legs. A physiotherapist, occupational therapist, or cranio-sacral therapist can help and advise with these exercises. It will be most beneficial to find a cranio-sacral therapist who has experience with and is good at treating children.

A child who has special problems with the sense of touch (that is, being touched), for example tactile shyness, requires a course of stimulation planned by a therapist. Massage and brush-massage are some of the methods the therapist can employ, but children born too early have a special sensitivity regarding being touched, and not all react positively to brushing.

A child who has had to live for a long period with SI problems may be so psychologically burdened by its great (and often futile) attempts at dealing with daily life, that it needs therapeutic support. This could, for example, be in the shape of sandplay therapy or NLP therapy.

Support for a child with ADHD or a related diagnosis should be arranged to suit the individual child. The primary approach could be by way of one's own doctor, the social worker, or the school doctor. The doctor will often prescribe *Ritalin* to reduce the symptoms, but it is possible to train the brain of a ADHD-child so the child gains better social and technical skills and more self-confidence and becomes better able to concentrate. (For further information about brain-training see the English version of www .mentalfitness.dk as well as www.corporate-psychology.net. Advice, guidance, and further information can be found at www.addiss .co.uk and, in the United States, at www.add-adhd.org.)

Delayed motor-skill development

The motor-skill problems may have significant psychological consequences for all age groups—for example, because the child finds it difficult to tie its shoelaces or do up its buttons—but that child is also always the last out to play and is never the first to be selected for the football team.

Hanne Agerholm (2003)

Causes and reactions

Children's motor-skill development continues generally up to the age of 8–10 years, and it is dependent upon the development in many different areas of the brain. Most motor-skill development problems are caused by retarded development or damage to the brain during the foetal period, at birth, or during the neonatal period (Trillingsgaard, Dalby, & Østergaard, 2003).

Most prematurely born children show delayed motor-skill development, be it gross motor skills or fine motor skills. In many instances the fine-motor-skill difficulties are the most visible and will therefore draw attention and be the reason for initiating an effort to remedy this. Difficulties in building with bricks, holding eating utensils, drawing, or writing are easier to discern than are difficulties with climbing, kicking, balance, and so on, because as a rule fine-motor-skill efforts result in a final product. However, the strength, stamina, and balance that is given by well developed gross-motor-skill function is the foundation for fine-motor-skill functions (Tóroddsdóttir, 2001).

Delayed motor-skill development can be caused partly by central nervous system, which is immature at birth, partly by inappropriate influence on the senses, and partly by deficient stimulation of senses and motor skills once outside the womb.

Motor-skill movements are the final link in the child's development, and they are thus linked to the sensory development that has preceded it, just as they develop further together with the senses while being supported by earlier experiences (Tóroddsdóttir, 2001). Frequently occurring difficulties in integrating the sense inputs are thus closely knitted to the motor difficulties that premature children may have.

These children can take a long time to sit up by themselves, to crawl, walk, run, ride a bicycle, climb, eat with knife, fork, or spoon, hold a pencil in the correct manner, build with bricks, tie shoelaces, and so on. The grasping reflex can be weaker and slower, and the bending impulse (which enables the child to curl up) may be missing.

Very prematurely born infants often have large, jerky movements and experience difficulties in changing easily from one type of movement to another. Tiny infants can easily develop a favoured side, which can result in bodily asymmetry.

A child born three months too early will normally only be able to maintain prolonged eye contact once it is four moths old, and be able to sit without support when it is about 10 months old.

The lack of stimulation of the sense of balance during the time in the womb and during the period spent in hospital can mean that the child later tries to avoid experiences that actually develop this sense and thus train important motor functions. The child would rather lie on its back than on its stomach and so does not practise lifting the head and upper body. It avoids rolling on the floor and crawling, or it only begins these late. It will only stand up once it feels totally stable on its legs. Once the child begins to walk, it finds it difficult to manage the freedom to move, and it may have an underdeveloped spatial concept. So now, having been reticent about moving out, it will run off and will be likely to run into objects (Tóroddsdóttir, 2001). This disparity between mental and motor-skill development is very often seen in toddlers that had been born too early. The child is mentally prepared for the next step in its development, but the motor skills are not ready. This can cause terrible frustration to the child.

Motor skills and language skills are connected, and delayed motor development can be contributory to language difficulties, including delayed language development, which is more frequent in premature children than in children born at term. Motor restlessness is very often observed in prematurely born children. Children with this restlessness are in continuous movement, they cannot sit quietly on a chair, they cannot stand still. One of the causes of this is the low muscle-tone of a child who was born much too soon and who did not have treatment with a physiotherapist or an occupational therapist, nor had cranio-sacral therapy.

The child has to use a disproportionate amount of energy to hold its body upright, and it is therefore forced to keep moving.

Many premature children lack "grounding". They show this by walking on their toes and by seeking out contact with the surface, both inside and outside. They very often lie on the floor, roll and turn, and generally move in a reclining position.

Prevention and remedies

As the infant grows, it develops more skills and functions. So only after the child is about 2 years old is it possible to evaluate its differentiated motor skills, perception, intellectual capacity, and language. The child develops and trains its motor skills by means of play, physical efforts, and other daily occupations; it is extremely important to give the child as many possibilities as possible to indulge in these activities and in general to ensure that it gets variation in physical activities—this also during early infancy.

In cases of motor problems without an ascertained neurological cause one can, for example, use the following procedure to elucidate and plan how to help:

1. Describe the problem and how this hampers the child socially and during play.
2. Judge if there is a need for general training or if there is only a need to focus on specific skills that need to be developed. Skills such as running and ball games have to be trained with focus on the actual function.
3. Train with the relevant difficult level of difficulty and give much positive feedback.

Swimming and horse riding provide general training, which, furthermore, has an added value in that the underdeveloped areas of the brain are trained. Riding trains and relaxes many muscle groups, being out in the countryside gives peace, a feeling of well-being and happiness, and mastering the required interaction between child and horse gives self-confidence. There is also an important social factor in riding. Through the horse's movement, the child's circulation, breathing, digestion, balance, motor function, walking/running patterns, coordination of the senses, ability to concentrate, head- and body control, as well as muscular strength, are all stimulated. Riding can also have a beneficial effect on spasticity. Swimming strengthens the child in most of the same areas as horse riding, but with gravity and skin stimulation as the most substantial elements.

A child born too early, with delayed motor development, will sooner or later achieve the necessary skills. The child should be given the chance to train and develop at its own pace, with full acceptance of the resultant delay. It is not always necessary to initiate treatment, but if this is considered necessary, then physiotherapy or occupational therapy as well as cranio-sacral therapy can help motor skills to develop. If the child is lacking in "earth connection", then massage, particularly of the lower part of the spine and under the feet (if the child will permit it), is beneficial.

Separation anxiety

We have all of us to some degree experienced a pang of pain by the separation at our birth. We came from security, warmth, and the sound of mother's heart out to face strong light, the cold, and separation from our source of safety and love, Mum. The fear of separation can be particularly strong if one was not quite ready to enter the world, did not get placed on Mum, and thus did not have eye and body contact, was exposed to various hospital treatments, placed into an incubator, or surrounded by fear that one would not survive, emanating from well-meaning people present.

Annette Petersen (2001, p. 19)

Causes and reactions

Many prematurely born children have a marked fear of being separated from, in particular, the mother, but it can also be from the father or both parents. During their first year they cling to their parents and cry fit to break one's heart if the parents leave them, even if they just leave the room. It can be incredibly difficult for the child to have to leave its parent in order to start at nursery, kindergarten, or school, and there will often be very few persons with whom the child feels sufficiently safe and confident and who can look after it.

If the child has had a traumatic start in life, been separated early from the mother, and has had a preponderance of negative emotional experiences, it will be anxious and insecure. When it is eventually able to build up a close feeling of security and trust—a symbiosis—with its mother, it will be the first secure experience since its time in the womb. It is therefore natural that it should fear a new separation, a new breach of faith, a new sorrow. This is one of the reasons why it clutches and clings to its mother (or father), and it is not unusual for this to continue right up to school age, though diminishing by degrees.

Not only insecurity with strangers, but also insufficient self-confidence and low self-esteem can cause the child to cling to this symbiosis, which prevents it from finding independence.

Generally a child will hide its strong reactions to the day's happenings at nursery or kindergarten until it sees one of its parents. At this point it often reacts by turning away in an attempt at mastering the strong emotions, and this can be followed by almost an explosion of reaction. The day's accumulated impressions and feelings are expressed when the child feels totally safe together with its parents.

In premature children these conditions may be extreme due to the facts mentioned above, as well as sensory-integration problems and delayed reactions.

Prevention and remedies

During early infancy it is important to give the child as much positive contact as possible: the kangaroo method, presence and closeness: everything that makes the child feel more safe will help it later to get rid of its clinging dependency on the parents. If the infant cries when left alone in the room for just a moment, it needs to know that Mum or Dad (or other person caring for it) will return in a moment. Even if the child is only a few months old, it will understand this message.

The first steps towards removing the fear of separation are taken when the child feels safe with its parents and a good interaction is established.

Following this, one can gradually make the child feel safe by introducing first one, and later more, adults.

Both anxiety and fear of separation can be good reasons to keep the child at home for a longer period. It will find it easier to attach itself to persons other than its parents if this happens gradually and at home.

The child will itself sense it own limitations in relation to other people, and its "no" to contact and any "yes" related to its own boundaries should be respected. The child has a need to progress through its developmental phases at its own pace, and it should be permitted its own feelings and senses of being ready—even if this does upset grandmother or auntie.

Once the child feels safe with friends and other family members, the parents can slowly move out of the picture, naturally paying attention to the child's reactions. It can be a long time be-tween the child's first acceptance of sitting with another adult and progressing to being content staying with family and friends.

If the child at nursery or institution finds it difficult to say goodbye to Mum and/or Dad, it is of great importance that at the moment of separation the child has close contact with an adult whom it trusts. Firm good-bye rituals assist in making the situation less threatening. It is also important to let the child know that Mum and Dad are coming back. Even though it is difficult to make such good-byes brief, that is best for the child.

Prolonged leave-taking adds to the difficulties—the child gradually becomes more and unhappy, because it is coming more and more into contact with the fear and insecurity and senses the parent's discomfort at leaving.

Infant therapy, sandplay therapy, and NLP therapy are recommended to help remedy the problem, because these tackle the root cause of the child's fears and feelings of betrayal.

Eating problems

The eating situation had developed into a grotesque performance with disappointed expectations, preconceived ideas about norms and good behaviour, and the fear that she was not getting sufficient nourishment.

Marianne Schledermann (2001, p. 21)

Causes and reactions

Eating problems are the norm rather than the exception with pre-mature children, but the shape and size of the problem vary greatly from one end of the scale to the other: from lack of wanting to eat to voracious appetite.

Children born much too early, with a low birth weight in rela-tionship to the week of birth (dysmature), may, in particular, have eating problems.

Eating problems can be:

— difficulties with digestion;

— pain in connection with and after eating;

— frequent gulping and vomiting;

— too little strength to suck sufficiently for long;

— lack of hunger sensations;

— lack of appetite, dislike of food, refusal to eat;

— difficulties in sucking, chewing, and swallowing;

— inability to feed oneself;

— lack of concentration;

— faddishness;

— voracious appetite.

Premature infants are underweight right from the start, and eating difficulties may mean that the child does not grow and gain weight as it should.

However, minor eating problems should not give cause for major worries. It is important that the child grows and gains in weight, but at its own pace. One cannot—and ought not—compare the growth and development of the child with children who are born full-term.

Weight, length, and head circumference should keep pace with each other. If the child is very ill or undernourished, it first loses weight, then the increase in height will slow down, and, finally, the head circumference will no longer increase. This does not happen very often, but when it does it is serious and demands observation and treatment by a physician.

Basic causes

The sucking/swallowing technique develops in tandem from about Week 30 onward. The coordination of the sucking/swallowing functions is only developed at about Week 34 in many children and for a few not before the time of birth (at term). This means that children born before this point will as a rule be unable to suck by themselves and must be given food via a nasal tube or cannula.

When the child is fed by nasal cannula, food is given regularly—for example, every second, third or fourth hour, depending on the child's age and size. This means that the child does not always feel hunger before it is fed, and this may have an impact on the child's ability to recognize hunger pangs later on—in some cases for several years.

Dysmaturity—that is, low birth weight in relation to birth week—can be a contributory factor to eating problems. A child who has received too little nourishment during the foetal period will often lack the feeling of satiation—"fullness". But this concerns primarily only those children who are born a little prematurely. A very prematurely born child, who has also weighed too little at birth, will very often lack the desire to eat.

The immature gastrointestinal system can be the cause of wind and poor digestion, and this can mean that the child suffers pain during the meal. This may be evident in several ways, but it is not uncommon that the infant is unable to force food down into a pain-burdened gastrointestinal system and refuses to eat any more, even though it is still hungry.

A comparatively small stomach—at a birth weight of 1 kg the size of a hazelnut—means that the child has a need to eat little, but often for a longer period. This, in conjunction with the underdevelopment in the gastrointestinal system and little strength due to little growth, as well as other problems, is the reason why every meal can take an incredibly long time, and be a less-than-elevating and happy experience for both parents and child.

Some children may have an anatomical obstruction—that is, a narrowing in the throat or gullet. Some premature children also suffer from a poorly functioning sphincter at the entry to the stomach (reflux).

A poor or delayed mouth-motor skill can make it difficult for the small infant to eat; this can include the ability both to suck and to eat from a spoon.

When a premature child gulps and dribbles a great deal, has continuing problems with sucking, swallowing, and chewing, spits out lumps and whole pieces of food, or vomits the food up, it may mean that the child will be diagnosed as having dysphagia:

impaired ability to swallow. The causes of dysphagia can be many, but with premature children it most often is caused by deficient development and function of the nerves and musculature (Russell, 1997).

The child may have negative experiences linked to mouth and throat, which can mean that it does not want to taste the food and it may lack interest in feeding itself. Some children are easily over-stimulated by too many impressions at table, and this can influence their desire to eat.

On the neonatal ward much emphasis is placed on weight and growth: everything is recorded on charts, and it can be difficult for parents to change from this once they are at home with the child. It can be hard to accept that the child does not eat at a meal, or that it only eats a little. One can become so fixated in the desire for the child to eat and gain weight that this becomes a mental and educational question. The problem can be further aggravated because the child continues to be of tiny stature and has difficulty gaining weight. Another psychological aspect of the lack of desire to eat can be the child's reaction to worn-out, unsure, powerless parents.

Children who have had eating and digestive problems from the beginning and who have been exposed to extended, disturbed, and demanding meals may develop special food habits.

Many premature infants suffer from constipation. This can be caused by iron supplements in the food, feeding with breast milk substitute, and/or an immature and badly functioning digestive system.

Abdominal pains can also occur in the slightly older child, actually right up to school age, and these can result in a lack of desire to eat. The pains can be caused by imbalance in the gastrointestinal system due to early birth, and they can be related to too little gastric juice. If the premature child has trapped neck vertebrae or other blockages in bones or joints, the digestive system is unlikely to function optimally.

Lack of appetite may mean that the child is not getting the necessary amount of proteins, carbohydrates, fat, minerals, and vitamins. This will lead to loss of weight or to not putting weight on, and it will also weaken the immune system. The child becomes tired and off-colour, which can further depress the appetite.

Some eating problems are caused by hypersensitivity or allergy. A child can be hypersensitive without having an allergy. Hypersensitivity cannot be diagnosed by means of blood test or other methods, but it can be identified by means of exclusion diets and exposure to the suspect foodstuffs. The exclusion method consists of removing certain foods from the child's diet for a period of time. Exposure treatment means that the child is given foodstuff and/or has those elements that are under suspicion of being the cause of hypersensitivity applied to the skin.

Frequently eating problems have more than one cause. If the child is overstimulated, insecure, frightened, sleeping badly, and has to fight against infections or illness, infected tonsils, and so on, it can lose the desire to eat. Social difficulties and general lack of growth can also lead to eating problems, just as neurological disturbances can have an influence.

Prevention and remedies

Infants

The most optimal is breastfeeding for a longer period. If this is not successful, one can get breast milk substitute that is suitable for premature infants, such as Prematil/Prenan until the child weighs about 2,500 g or has reached full-term size, followed by Aptamil First until the child weighs about 4 kg. The premature infant milk substitutes contain a higher proportion of protein, calcium, phosphorus, and calories, and they have added N3 and N6 fatty acids (long-chain polyunsaturated), which are of special importance to the child's growth and development, including the brain and central nervous system. In some countries it is possible to apply for a refund of the expenses incurred by using the special milk substitutes.

If the child gulps great deal or actually vomits its food up, one can try to change to another brand of breast milk substitute. Enfamil *AR* (anti reflux) is specially developed for this purpose. It can also help if carob-bean flour is added to the food to thicken it so that it does not pass upward so easily in the gastrointestinal system. Breastfed children can be given a teaspoonful of porridge consisting of a boiled mixture of 3% carob-bean flour and water before the feed. Children who are not breastfed can be given boiled carob-bean flour in the bottle in the following concentration:

— 0.5 g (= 1 ml) to 100–150 ml breast milk substitute;

— 0.5 g (= 1 ml) to 200 ml maize porridge.

Cold water and the flour are whipped together, and the mixture is boiled up, while being beaten; it is left to cool to 40°, and the milk powder is then added. It should have the consistency of a thick sauce.

In time the gastrointestinal system will mature, and the child will eventually grow out of gulping, vomiting, and pain in connection with meals. The child does not swallow air when it is being spoon-fed, and the mobility once it gradually begins to crawl and walk stimulates the digestive system.

The infant's constipation can sometimes be eased by altering the supplementary amount of liquid iron. The number of drops given can be reduced, or the drops can be given throughout the course of the day instead of being given in one dose. It may be possible to stop giving the iron supplement entirely—the surgery nurse or the doctor will be able to judge. Adding juice of figs to the food can help alleviate constipation. Lactulose and Laxoberal drops are often prescribed and may be necessary to break the vicious cycle, but one must be aware that these are produced chemically. Movicol is a new product, recently given the go-ahead for use for children. There are also several natural products that stimulate the intestinal function, and one can always ask for help from the pharmacist.

Transition to solids

Infants are generally ready to change to solid food by the age of about five months. The premature child's gastrointestinal system adapts more rapidly to being able to absorb solid food outside the womb, and this means that as a rule the infant can begin to take solid food when it is about half-way between the actual birth date and five months from the time of being full-term. However, even though the gastrointestinal system is ready, it is not certain that the mouth motor skills are. If the child has great difficulty in getting food off the spoon, into the mouth, and further on down, then one ought to wait a little longer before spoon-feeding.

Colds, constipation, thrush, or teething can all inhibit the child's ability and desire to eat.

If the child is of low weight with a nonoptimally functioning gastrointestinal system, there may be a need for heightened awareness at the changeover from breast/bottle feeding to more solid food.

Some suggestions (from Dietician Lisbeth Skafte, Hvidovre Hospital, Denmark) are:

— acidified Allomin + 2–3% maize flour (to thicken the consistency);
— acidified Allomin + whipping cream (10 ml/100 ml milk);
— thin porridge + acidified Allomin 1:1;
— NAN 2 Probiotic supplementary mixture with lactic acid bacteria (to ensure growth of beneficial gut bacteria);
— maize or millet porridge in the bottle or by spoon.;
— puréed potato and carrot ±2 tsp. vegetable fat;
— puréed fruit (pear, kiwi fruit, peach, apple).

It can be easier for the child to become acquainted with the spoon if, to begin with, it is always the same type of food that is offered. Tiny spoonfuls give the child a better chance of keeping up with the feed. Once the child has become used to the soft and light thin porridge fed by spoon, one can progress to porridge or a maize or millet porridge of a more substantial consistency, which are filling and good for the digestion. The porridge can be made with expressed breast milk or mother's milk substitute.

The book market offers much literature about infant nutrition, some also containing recipes and methods. For children who have problems with sucking, swallowing, and chewing, look for literature about "dysphagia" (much information and many suggestions for infant and child nutrition are given on www.herbalremedies.com/herremforchi.html).

Older children

An infant that is low in weight and has difficulties in gaining weight needs substantial vitamins, proteins, carbohydrates, and fats. The optimal solution will be to offer healthy, nourishing, and varied food, with masses of fruit and vegetables. Legumes contain just about all the most important food substances. Avocado, banana, dried fruits, nuts, vegetable oil, porridge, and coarse bread together combine to make a good basic diet.

Food that is too monotonous and too refined can be a contributory cause of allergic or hypersensitive reactions.

Premature children who find it difficult to chew, suck, and swallow may need mashed and lump-free food for a longer period than normal. The necessary supplements should be added, taking the child's age into consideration. A good rule of thumb is: taste according to age, and consistency (of food) according to the level of functionality. As a rule, the older the child is, the stronger and more varied the tastes it will like.

If one offers regular, firm mealtimes and avoids between-meal consumption of sugar-rich and highly refined stimulants without nourishment value, the child can be helped to have a healthy relation to food and to mealtimes. It also has a positive effect on the digestive system and the body balance in general.

Children who suffer from constipation should avoid white bread and other food with low fibre content. White bread sticks to the intestines and irritates the mucous membranes. Lightly boiled or baked vegetables are easier to digest than are raw ones.

Both young and older constipated children need much liquid—preferably water—and not taken with meals, because the liquid dilutes the digestive juices and thus inhibits the digestive process.

If the problem with constipation is very marked and comprehensive, then professional help is needed, as there can be a matter of obstruction (*obstipation*), which should be treated. One must in general pay attention to the whole of the child's prehistory, including the neonatal period, diet, and changes of ingredients, when and how the problems began, and any special circumstances connected with this. The child's mental condition as well as its attitude to using the lavatory and its lavatorial habits can also play a significant role.

If a child has problems with low blood-sugar levels, an orange or a handful of raisins can quickly balance things up. Raisins contain fibre and are therefore also good for the digestion. The carbohydrate contents give energy to the brain and muscles. Some raisins have been treated with sulphur and added sugar, and these should be avoided.

Most children have periods of reduced appetite and marked choosiness. A child whose reduced appetite is due to an infection needs a great amount of energy while avoiding overloading the digestive system. This can be achieved by means of liquid food with a good energy content, such as vegetable soup, bouillon, vegetable juice, and fruit juice, as well as unsweetened curdled milk products such as yogurt or cottage cheese.

The required extra proteins can be found in quark, soy curds, nuts, eggs, and fish. Food supplements can be of benefit.

In cases of allergy we are talking about completely individual advice regarding diet, and this must be given by a doctor and/or a dietician. But healthy homemade food will always be a better choice than industrially produced ready-made meals.

Education and psychology at mealtimes

Mealtimes are not just about eating, but to a great extent also about contact and care. If mealtime is a time of worry as well as mental games and unsure teaching methods, then it is worthwhile stopping and trying to view it all from an outsider's perspective.

A talk with the surgery nurse or with other parents of premature children, as well as looking at literature dealing with child psychology and education in connection with mealtimes, can be what is needed to break the cycle and progress with less stress and more relaxation at mealtimes.

Some general and relevant suggestions can be to avoid letting the mealtimes take too long, not to press or force the child to eat or taste, and not to threaten with punishment or tempt with rewards. Those methods can exacerbate the eating problems and give the child an inappropriate attitude to food and mealtimes.

The child should be permitted to feed itself, even if it does make a mess. It has a need to explore its food, to train its fine motor skills and experience that it can do it by itself. In fact, the chance of early exploration of the food can increase the child's desire for food, and it can be an important foundation to avoid later choosiness or faddishness.

Consistency is an important concept in relation to meals, just as it is with normal upbringing. If the child is offered a comparatively broad selection of healthy food, including fresh, good bread, then there will always be something that the child likes and fancies eating, and in this way the food cannot be used to exert moral pressure on the adults.

If the child still tries to put pressure on its parents, one can with a clear conscience say that it must eat something from the table, and that nothing else will be served. If the child, in playing psychological game, does not eat much at a single mealtime, then hunger will ensure that this is caught up at the following meal.

The atmosphere in connection with meals plays a significant part. If the adults show that they enjoy preparing, cooking, and/or eating food and that they enjoy the time spent together during the meal, then this becomes a positive experience for the child. Even if the adults and the child do not eat the same type of food, it is important that they eat together.

If a child is overstimulated by the many visual, taste, touch, and sound impressions at the table, it may help to remove everything other than the child's mug and plate from the table and to use a nonstimulating, plain tablemat or cloth, preferably in a pastel colour, and also to avoid background noise and other things that could stimulate the senses.

Arranging the food so it looks appetising and delicious can help to stimulate the child's appetite. One can also offer the food one small portion at a time, so that the child will be better able to gain an overview of the meal and one can ensure that the food is easy to chew and swallow. If the child does not get a feeling of being full, it needs to be given carefully weighed portions.

Some specific preventative actions

Parents' societies both in Denmark and in Norway have noted that children whose tonsils have been removed have an increased appetite following the operation. The tonsils can make it difficult for the child to swallow, and it follows that the child will eat less.

Infant therapy and sandplay therapy can ease stress build-up in the child and can also help to relieve the early mental experiences that can have an influence on appetite.

Cranio-sacral therapy can also release pent-up stress, just as it can improve the digestion and regulate the appetite.

It is possible to get food supplements, which can help in cases of lack of appetite, and nutritional supplements can be justified in this case. Pains that are caused by lack of gastric juice can be alleviated by stimulation of the gastric juices by nonchemical food supplements.

It is not only dysmature children who can have a good appetite right from the start. Premature children who have an undisturbed daily routine, have love, care, security, good sleep, protection against infection and overstimulation as well as against unnecessary treatment—in short, children who are thriving—will as a rule also have a good appetite.

Language difficulties

Dance, rhythm, and use of the body were also a part of Maria's culture, which she used a lot together with the children. This meant that Charlotte learned an incredible number of songs, and this was, among other things, helpful in developing her language very quickly at the same time as her motor skills were trained.

Gitte Fedderholdt (2002, p. 9)

Causes and reactions

Language difficulties in children born too early can show as delayed speech or problems with understanding language and speech. Many premature children are rather slow to learn to speak, and some of them will at some point have need of a speech therapist. A proportion of these children—including those born very much too early—do manage without any problems, however.

The centre for speech in the brain is under the influence of immaturity at birth and the inappropriate conditions for development outside the womb.

Late motor-skill development is also contributory to language difficulties, just as repeated middle-ear infections or fluid in the middle ear can hamper language development.

When the speech therapist judges how the child can be helped towards more fluent language, a distinction is made between *speech impediment* and *language difficulties.*

Speech impediment relates to superficial mistakes in speech where the child finds it difficult to pronounce certain sounds but has a normal command of language otherwise.

Language difficulty is more deep-rooted because it concerns difficulties in understanding how language functions—understanding a message and formulating language.

A child with language difficulties does not necessarily have any difficulties with pronunciation. One can only expect a premature child to speak properly once it is 4–5 years old. A speech therapist can provide information about children's general development of language, including when one can expect that the child will have developed the necessary skills.

If the child finds it difficult to make itself understood, this can affect its self-confidence, with which premature children may already have problems.

The language of twins or triplets is often slow in developing. If this is the case, the first words will be uttered later, the children will express themselves using shorter sentences, and they will have a smaller vocabulary. Their language can, in some cases, demand extra attention, especially if they develop their own language to communicate between themselves or if one speaks for the other(s). Children from multiple births may have their own language, consisting of a simplification of normal language sounds: they may, occasionally, invent their own words for some things.

Prevention and remedies

Speech impediment does not, as a rule, need any extra professional contribution, but language development can be optimized by means of a little daily help in the shape of rhymes and jingles or nursery rhymes, conversation, story reading, as well as exercises that train the motor skills, including normal physical activity. Rhythmic movement to jingles, nursery rhymes, and/or music is a good combination for language development stimulation. Sensorimotor exercises will equally assist in this development.

Infant massage and parent/child gymnastics can also help towards better language development. Bouncing on a trampoline activates most of the muscles in the body—including the muscles the child uses for speaking.

If the child speaks while bouncing on a trampoline it finds it easier to find the right intonation, and the sounds become more distinct than when the child is sitting quietly in a chair. At the same time, trampoline-bouncing strengthens the sense of balance and gross motor development, which are both significant prerequisites for good language.

Play where the child uses and focuses on the lips, tongue, and palate strengthens the mouth motor skills and thus the ability for proper enunciation. These can be, for example, using a straw to blow a piece of cotton-wool on the table, eating food that has to be chewed really carefully, licking food or crumbs from the mouth, or eating small pieces of food without using the hands.

But the child first and foremost develops its language by talking with others, children as well as adults, and so it is an important parental task to chat a great deal with one's child every day. As a good "language model" one must ensure clear formulation and simple sentences, and make sure that the communication is suited to the child's level. The message should be short, clear, and unambiguous. To help to stimulate the understanding of language, one can ask questions that require an answer, give positive responses to the child's statements, and expand and lengthen the child's sentences. During play, language is used and developed considerably, so the opportunity should be taken to help the child by entering its games. One should avoid correcting the child's language and, instead, repeat words or sentences in correct terms. For example, if the child says: "Look, I land on my tummy!" the adult replies "Yes I can see you landed on your tummy—was it fun?" In this way the child is not rebuked but is helped to learn the correct syntax.

It is good to place demands on the child's level of language and conversation. The family soon learns to understand the child's sounds and body language and may get into the habit of reacting to these. It will help the child's language development if the family insists on the child using the correct words to communicate.

The language of twins (and other multiple-birth children) can be influenced by their closeness and fellowship. If one finds that a twin is talking for the other, one should help the children to break this pattern. The method will be dependent upon the children and the individual situation, but it can be done by, for example, not acknowledging the communication, separating the children for a few hours every day, teaching them to take turns in speaking, and starting conversations or addressing questions to the child who does not speak for itself. If the quiet and less talkative child needs extra attention because to language difficulties, one must be aware that the other child needs compensation for the added attention its sibling is having.

If the twins develop their own language, one should optimize language stimulation as a daily routine, both by reading for and talking a great deal with the children and by having each child alone with the adult part of the time. Twins' language development is discussed specifically in books about twins.

Premature children may need help to overcome persistent problems with language understanding and speech. It is possible to contact a speech therapist through the surgery nurse, the child's doctor in the children's outpatient ward, the clinic, day nursery, or school.

There are various educational possibilities for children with speech or language difficulties. Some speech therapists work with the child on a one-to-one basis, while others gather the children in groups. Regardless of the method, it is important to make an early start, which means from about age of 4. Research has shown that there is a connection between language difficulties and later difficulties with reading and writing.

As in the main language difficulties are caused by the brain's immaturity and unfavourable conditions during the time immediately after birth, physiotherapy or occupational therapy as well as cranio-sacral therapy may help to alleviate the problem partially or totally or.

If there is uncertainty about the child's level of language development, a broad-spectrum test system and/or a speech therapist can give a more concrete evaluation, just as books about children and language development give guidance for the normal pattern of children's language development.

A grommet in the ear or other treatment can be most beneficial for language development if the child has ear problems.

Ten concrete suggestion for language training in daily life (Rouw, 1997)

1. Put words to your actions.
2. Read aloud.
3. Sing songs.
4. Play with the language.
5. Turn off the radio and television.
6. Show what letters are used for.
7. Talk about language.
8. Give yourself time.
9. Answer the child's questions.
10. Use the library.

Stress and restlessness

The earlier one has been exposed to stress—this can be during the foetal period through Mum's secretion of stress hormones and/or after too early a birth with consequent hospitalization on the neonatal ward—the worse a starting point one has for being able to handle stress later!

Helle Gram (2001, p. 25)

Causes and reactions

The child who was born much too early is exposed to stress before, during, and after birth. As early as in the early infantile period one can in some cases observe over-tense muscles caused by stress build-up in the body.

The underdeveloped central nervous system and immature brain make the child hypersensitive, and therefore very easily stressed. Infant massage, for instance, is too violent a stimulant for a very tiny child. In the infant stage, after the hospitalization, a very premature child is still easily stressed and overstimulated. In fact, stress and overstimulation are closely related concepts, but one of the main differences is that stress can also be caused by struggle—struggle for nourishment, struggle against infection, struggling to survive.

Stress causes restlessness, which can manifest itself in restless sleep and continuous body movement. As infants, premature children often have a great need to be active for the greater part of their waking time. They can find it difficult to toddle about and to play alone.

If the child has a reduced ability to function because of, for example, sensory-integration problems, a poor memory, language difficulties, delayed motor-skill development, as well as fear and insecurity, it is suffering massive stress in its daily life, which can result, for instance, in tension in the body, headache and stomach ache, mental and emotional disturbance, motor restlessness, aggressiveness, or withdrawal. Characteristically, boys tend on the whole to react to stress in an extrovert manner, while girls most frequently react by becoming withdrawn (Zlotnik, 2001).

Prevention and remedies

Symptoms of stress and restlessness, just like hyperactivity, can be a reaction to overstimulation, and more or less the same rules for help are common for all. A firm routine in daily life is important. The child must have tranquil and secure surroundings, associate with small groups of people, and not be exposed to too many impressions and experiences.

Too many toys and strong colours can be overstimulating and cause agitation. It is possible to stimulate the child's body into movement exclusively by means of the senses, by which means one establishes peace, concentration, and close contact.

It is secure and relaxing for the child to be in a cave or nest. Right after the stay in the incubator, one can build a nest of cloth nappies or other soft material, so that the child senses the boundaries. One will often note that for many years premature children tend to love to snuggle in nests and caves.

Music can act as stress relief. In the incubator the child can listen to music from a Walkman or Discman (disinfected). New-age music, quiet classical music, dolphin sounds, and heartbeat are preferable. However, music can, in some cases, induce stress, so it is important that the child is kept under observation for stress and overstimulation, particularly if it is listening to music in the incubator.

Later on the child can have great pleasure in having a daily half-hour de-stressing to music—preferably the possibly familiar music from the time in the incubator.

If one lacks inspiration, the number *Wayfarer* by Kim Skovbye, or the pieces *Inner Harvest, One Fine Morning, Sweet Baby Dreams, Slumberland,* and *Blue Flame,* all from Fønix Music, are suggestions. Enya's songs and music can also be recommended.

"Transitions"—soothing music composed especially for unborn children and infants of 0 to 6 months—is music created on a synthesizer combined with sounds from the womb: breathing, heartbeat, and the sound of blood circulating. The CD *Transitions—Soothing Music for Mother and Baby* from the United States (produced by Transitions Music) can be recommended.

There are several interesting studies that show that different instruments influence different areas of the mind and body. For example, drums may give a better "earth connection", guitar music can influence pulse, heart, and solar plexus, and flute music as well as popular music can restore mind and body (Jørgensen, 1996).

The child can get help to calm physical unrest by means of close bodily contact—for example, with the use of a sling or by infant massage, as well as quiet activities and immersion in, say, a story, a drawing, or a quiet, imaginative game.

The time spent daily at an institution should not be too long, This applies also to older children with stress symptoms. Free-time arrangements will as a rule be too much for the child for whom it is an effort just to get through the school day. The change to after-school care arrangements, with new rules, new children and adults, new activities, and many people gathered together can have a great impact, and the day can be much too long, with too many impressions and demands.

Prematurely born children can benefit from horse riding, swimming, gymnastics, trampolining, self-defence, and so on, but the time spent on free-time activities should be limited. The child has a need for time at home doing nothing, caring for itself, or being with the family in peaceful and relaxing conditions. It is also under these conditions that the chance arises for a good chat and bonding. It is to a great extent a parental responsibility to manage the child's time so the daily routine does not become too hectic. Included in this is, of course, also the management of the parent's own time, so one can be calm and not worn out and stressed. The child is positively influenced by a parental low stress level.

Some of the causes of stress lie, as is known, in the child's inability to integrate its sense impressions, and this can be alleviated by means of the ball blanket and/or ball cushion, physiotherapy or occupational therapy, and cranio-sacral therapy; the latter two can also positively influence muscle tension. By means of simple techniques, one can help the child to relax. Physiotherapists or occupational therapists can give advice on this.

Regular and plentiful sleep, peace and stability in everyday life, good diet, physical exertion, care, and good social contact all help to reduce stress levels.

Sleep problems

When night finally came, she only settled down if she lay on top of me, with her face towards my heart. I had to be there with bodily contact before she was secure enough to relax. Even then she woke between 13 and 16 times every night and cried fit to break your heart.

Signe Merete Hyld (2003, p. 24)

Causes and reactions

Many full-term children have sleep problems during infancy, and some of these can appear similar to, or be identical with, sleep problems premature children may have. Very premature children's sleeping patterns do show, however, some common characteristics.

Sufficient routine-filled, quiet sleep is essential for the brain's and body's chances of self-restoration and thus for the child's development and growth. Prematurely born children have extra need of help for development and growth, and that is why it is worrying that sleep problems occur so often.

The child may be frightened to fall asleep. It appears as though the child feels that it is unsafe to sleep. It is easy to find the reason: in the past sleep has been interrupted by unpleasant and painful treatments as well as sudden loud noises from the technical equipment.

The child's fundamental fear and insecurity from the traumatic start in life is active in the subconscious.

It is also very common that premature children only sleep for a few hours during the day and that they sleep very lightly and are very easily awakened, particularly by sudden loud noises. During the neonatal period the child has been exposed to many shocks and abrupt awakening. Furthermore the brain was insufficiently developed at birth to control the stages of REM/non-REM deep and light sleep.

It is often noted that premature children are frightened of the dark. On the neonatal ward the light is left on day and night—even though it presumably is dimmed during the night—and so during its first few months of life the child has not known total darkness. thus the dark can induce fear, as it is a new phenomenon and at the same time represents an uncertainty factor in that it is not palpable and therefore in the child's consciousness may be hiding danger.

The child can therefore have a great need to be close to Mum and/or Dad at bedtime and, for that matter, all the time it is sleeping. Many premature children settle best when they are either lying on the stomach of one of its parents or are embraced.

But sleep problems are not always over even if some of these arrangements induce the child to sleep. Many premature children waken many times during the night, and when awake, crying and panic stricken after a nightmare, it can be difficult or almost impossible to make contact with and to reach them. These night terrors have presumably the same origin as the child's fear of going to sleep, as mentioned above.

If children awaken insecure and crying, they have, as a rule, a need for contact with the parents, either because they feel that they have not had sufficient close contact or because they have had too many experiences during the day.

Children with SI problems—who often are very sensitive children—are very easily overstimulated during the day by impressions and experiences. They do not have the time to work through this while awake, so the brain is working under pressure during sleep to put all the impressions in the right places. A child whose senses are overstimulated will at the same time experience tension in its body, which will, together with the brain's increased level of activity, cause so much agitation that the child wakens.

The child can find it difficult to fall asleep not only in the evening and at night, but also for the afternoon nap. In fact, there may be much crying and screaming in connection with sleep problems. It is a cry for help from the child, but it can be rather difficult for the parents to detect what the child needs, and this gives rise to a vicious cycle. Continuous screaming can unnerve even the most composed adult, and the adult's helplessness and stress is transmitted to the child, who becomes even more upset and frustrated.

The child feels, and is influenced by, Mum and Dad's emotions, worry and uncertainty as well as happiness, tranquillity, and determination.

Sleep problems have a basis in several things simultaneously—for example, eating problems, teething, growing pains, infections, fluid in the middle ear (the child will not lie down) or other illness, as well as insecure and unsettled conditions in daily life.

Older children can also have sleep problems. They beginning to register and accept things in their existence that may have troubled them, and just as the premature children often have fundamental fears, so older children may be more influenced by their experiences than children normally are.

Children can find it difficult to sleep in unfamiliar places all through the preschool age. Just different surroundings and circumstances can give the child problems in dropping off to sleep, but things can get even more difficult if Mum or Dad is not there. A pair of beloved grandparents may possibly ensure that child has the necessary peace and security, but nursery outings with overnight stays and camping out with the school can be incredibly difficult for an insecure premature child.

Prevention and remedies

As many sleep problems in premature children are based on insecurity, overstimulation, and early traumatic experiences, security must be enhanced in everyday life and overstimulation avoided.

Security is enhanced if the child is surrounded in its bed: particularly head, bottom, and feet need to feel boundaries, for example in the shape of rolled-up cloth nappies or baby blankets.

Tucking-up rituals are very important for security. Old-fashioned advice to let the child lie on its own and scream cannot be put into practice, particularly not with premature children. If they show a need to be close to the parents during sleep, then one can be fairly sure that it is a genuine need, not an attempt to win a power game. A place in the double bed is naturally the prime solution for the child, but during the first year a safer solution is to have the child's cot or cradle standing right next to the bed, within touching distance.

Many premature children find it easiest to drop off to sleep when they are cradled in Mum or Dad's arms, preferably while walking. This can be strenuous for longer periods, and parents of premature children have found many creative solutions: for instance, to swing the child in a sheet, to bring the pram into the living-room, rock it up and down, and drive it forwards and backwards, or to make a hammock out of a child's duvet, which is tied together at both ends and hung up over the parent's double bed. The hammock can be kept in movement by one foot and thus one has the hands free to do something else.

If one can get one of these methods to work, it has the advantage that there is no need to move the child from the arms to the cradle or the cot, which may easily waken it.

It is naturally important to ensure the necessary safety precaution when one makes use of homemade methods.

If the child finds it difficult to sleep because of too much wind in the stomach, it can help to take the child in one's arms so that it lies with its stomach towards the adult's hand and arm and in this position the stomach can be massaged very gently.

Premature children may have a greater-than-usual need to suck. They can be helped to get to sleep if they have a dummy or a bottle with water or camomile tea (without sugar) in bed. The tea has a soothing effect.

As milk creates mucus in the mouth and throat, a little time must elapse between the last drink of milk and tucking in the child.

If the child has a cold, it will ease the pressure in the head if the headrest is raised—for example, with a pillow under the mattress or a couple of books under the legs of the bed.

Quiet music (see also under "Stress and restlessness") can also help the child to drop off to sleep.

Regarding overstimulation as a cause of sleep problems, it is essential to bear in mind that the experiences, impressions, and activities of the day accumulate, and then during the evening and/or the night the child becomes agitated and upset. For this reason the child needs a quiet, rhythmic day, with many small rest periods. These pauses or breaks act as small oases for where the child can digest the day's happenings bit by bit, so they do not accumulate.

Physiotherapy or occupational therapy, as well as cranio-sacral therapy, may help the child to find it easier to accept and work through sense-impressions and thus become less stimulated. These forms of treatment can also contribute to better sleep by means of muscle relaxation, which reduces the levels of stress.

A ball blanket (Brummerstedt, 2001; see also www.rompa.com) can help the child to damp down the sense impressions so it is able to relax, fall asleep, and stay asleep.

The time before the tucking-in ritual ought to be quiet and low-key. A warm bath, bodily contact with rocking movements, quiet music, and storytelling or listening can soothe and calm the child.

The child has a need of secure, firm fixed points at bedtime. Rituals form a part of these, but the boundaries in the bed and the bedroom are also of significance. The child should be able to see familiar things, it should have its dummy and its most loved cuddly soft toy in the bed. The bottle with water or camomile tea could also be an important aid to sleeping. Dimmed lights, light colours on the walls, not too many disturbing patterns, and things in their right place give a feeling of security and calm.

The child can be frightened and insecure if it wakes in a different place from where it fell asleep. If the child drops off to sleep at the breast, this will be what it will seek the instant it wakes.

If the family stays away from home overnight, it is important to create a feeling, an atmosphere, of security in the new surroundings.

An extra effort at avoiding infections and the resulting consequent illnesses may also help to ease eventual sleep problems. A healthy and suitable indoor climate (no more than 18° at night) plays a role in this connection, but is in any case a significant prerequisite for a good night's sleep. It is naturally important that the child is neither hungry nor overfed when it goes to sleep, just as it is very important that the digestion is working properly. Massage is a help to digestion and it sooths and relaxes. It is important to let the child (as far as possible) find its own sleep rhythm if it finds it difficult to go to sleep during the day. Rituals are just as essential during the day as they are in the evening. If the child has an afternoon nap in day care or in an institution, it may be necessary to make special arrangements—for example, that the child sleeps somewhere very quiet, that it has its own blanket, its own cuddly toy and/or something else from home, that there is an adult with the child whom it trusts, or that it is given a comforting bottle.

If the sleep problem worsens and results in violent crying and perplexed parents, it may be a good idea to take a little break. If one cannot help the child because one does not know what to do, then it may be best for both parties for the adults to withdraw in order to have a break from the unhappy situation and a chance to control thoughts and emotions. It will be beneficial if the other parent or another caring person who is close to the child can take over in the meantime. In fact, it will very often be necessary to take it in turns to put the child to bed and get it to sleep and to be available if it wakes during the night. The parent's self-confidence and consistency are just as important factors as are empathy and awareness of the child's needs. If the child's signals are noted and understood and it thus gets the right help to sleep, it becomes secure, gains confidence to trust the world, and finds it easier to leave the parents when that time comes.

The older child

Much motor activity and fresh air during the day is a good and natural aid to falling asleep.

When the time has come for the child to move away from the double bed and into its own room, the surroundings and circumstances are naturally important. Sleeping in a room together with siblings can make the child feel more secure. It can also be a solution if one of the parents sleeps on a mattress on the floor in the child's room.

When the slightly older child finds it difficult to drop off to sleep, it is an indication that it is still in need of peace, security, and rituals.

The child's by now expanded consciousness and recognition means that experiences influence the mind more. The child has a need for a secure, close, loving relationship where it is listened to and taken seriously, so that it does not lie alone with its thoughts in the evening.

It can be of assistance to the child to incorporate a revision of the day's activities into the goodnight ritual. The events are then in place in the child's consciousness, and any worries can be discussed and thus lessened or even eliminated.

Sometimes the child's fundamental fear creates a spontaneous anxiety that something bad is hiding in the bedroom. The child needs then to have the light turned on, to look in all the nooks and corners together with Mum or Dad, and perhaps go for a little evening walk in order to become familiar with the outdoor night sounds.

If the child has repeated nightmares of the same type, it means that it is struggling with something in the deeper layers of consciousness, which it needs help to resolve. During the actual nightmare the child will benefit by sleeping close to one of the parents. The following day it could draw the dream, and the scary figures can be made harmless by the drawing being torn into small pieces, being burnt, or the figures being redrawn to represent funny, benevolent creatures. But often it is the early traumas and fears from the hospital period of children born much too early that are expressed in the dreams, and it can require professional help in the shape of, for example, infant therapy or sandplay therapy in order to banish them.

If the premature child feels insecure when it has to spend a night in a strange place—say, for an outing arranged by the kindergarten or school—it must have total trust in the adult primary contact person.

A good interaction between parents and educator/teacher can ensure that the child's special need for security is fulfilled. The older preschool- or schoolchild will the able to express its needs, but often only to those adults whom it trusts 100%, and this will generally be the parents. Because of this there may still be a need for communication between home and institution regarding outings that include staying overnight. If the challenge is too great for the child, it may be necessary to keep the child at home. Just like motor development, so mental development must take place at a pace that the child can follow. If it has too much fear and insecurity to handle while sleeping away from home, then this should be postponed until the child does feel secure and ready.

NOTE

1. Questions to psychologist Lisbeth Gath; see under "Fagpanel" (http://praematur.dk).

CHAPTER THREE

Prevention
and possible treatment methods

When deciding who will be best suited to help treat the child's problems, selection should be based both upon experience and empathy in working with children. Experience with premature children is naturally an extra advantage, and obviously, a solid professional expertise in the subject is necessary.

The majority of the treatment methods described in this book are recognized by and integrated into the health services of most Western countries.

Only treatment methods that have been used frequently during the last five years or so in the alleviation of premature children's short- and long-term consequences of early birth have been selected. Selection was based on the evidence of countless communications by parents, communications in the journal of the Danish Premature Society, on the Society's homepage and on overseas premature Societies' homepages. Many reports have been collected at lectures given in Denmark and Norway.

In this section a series of aids that can be of value to premature children are also described.

Physiotherapy and occupational therapy

While the health visitor offers to visit as early as on the neonatal ward, the parents are only offered visits by the child ergo therapists once they have returned home from hospital and established a routine with the child. . . . At the visit the starting point is based on those problem areas that one knows from experience can arise in connection with premature children's motor and sensory development.

P. Tuxen and B. Filstrup (2002, p. 12)

The way the Danish Councils and hospitals use physiotherapists and occupational therapists (ergo therapists), respectively, is up to the individual authority: in practice there is not a great deal of difference between the two subject areas. The important thing with regard to a premature child is the therapist's insight as well as to identify with the child's situation and to find its resources. This is fundamental to working with the child's eventual problem areas.

At a sensorimotor evaluation the physiotherapist or occupational therapist primarily evaluates the child's muscle and joint position sense, sense of touch, balance, and vision. The quality of the movements and the child's ability to carry out movements that cross the body's centre-line are examined. Further, the child's ability to develop motor-skill strategies is evaluated. The therapist then decides on the extent of help required and works out an individual programme for the child.

A series of standardized tests—for example, AIMS (Alberta Infant Motor Scale), MPU (Motor Perceptual Development), MAP (Miller Assessment for Preschoolers), and Movement ABC (Assessment Battery for Children)—are available. Regardless of which test is used, it is important that it is repeated several times in order to evaluate the child's development over time.

Physio- and occupational therapy in particular can be used for training of motor skills and sensory integration. The SI function is of great meaning for the child's consciousness, perception, and sensorimotor development. Sensory-integration training is motor-skill and sensory training that aims at improving the brain's processing and organizing of sensory impressions.

During the training, work is focused especially on the stimulation of the senses of touch, balance, and muscle and joint sense, and the child is occupied for a long period of time in activities that challenge and stimulate its balance-, speed-, height-, and spatial perception (Tóroddsdóttir, 2001). It is the process and the experience that are important, and the fact that there is no pressure to perform well during the training really suits most premature children. The process should be experienced as a game that gives the child pleasure, and it should support the child's creativity, courage, and self-confidence.

Some general exercises for that are good for the stimulation of the senses and motor skills as well as points on how to avoid overstimulation are given below.

The infant

- Arranging the child's cot so that head, feet, and back are surrounded by pillows or rolls of blankets helps the child to assimilate input from its senses (touch, balance, muscle, and joint position senses) and to find peace and security.
- Placing the child on its side, changing between right and left sides, preferably with a rolled-up cloth nappy between the legs, can prevent bodily asymmetry; and it is beneficial to place the child in the foetal position, as this will improve the child's ability to bend its body.
- Preventing the "frog position"—knees bent and apart and feet turned out—when placing the child on its back by supporting arms and legs in a slightly bent position.
- Always using calm movements.
- Letting the child lie on its side and placing a hand, a cloth nappy or a piece of material on the child while it is being washed and changed; in this position the child feels embraced, encompassed, and more secure.
- Touching the tender premature child with a firm, flat hand—stroking movements and baby massage can overstimulate the newborn child, but can be excellent once the child is older.
- Rolling the child when it has to be turned from back to stomach and back again, in order to strengthen symmetry and body image.

— Bathing the child with a cloth nappy wrapped around the body in order to give it a feeling of being contained and encompassed, possibly in a narrow bath so the child can feel the boundaries.

— Letting the child lie on its stomach on sheepskin in order to stimulate its sense of touch (only when the child is awake); a groundsheet or aerobic training mats can also be used.

— Placing the child on its stomach on one's own breast to train it to lift its head and to give it bodily contact.

— "Cross-training" at the nursing table: right arm and left leg are moved towards each other, then the other two limbs; this is repeated until the child indicates that it has had enough. Cross-training assists coordination between the right and left hemispheres of the brain, a function that the child will need when it has to learn to crawl and later develop other motor skills, as well as when it has to perceive and integrate sensory impressions.

— Rocking the child, both while embracing it and when it is lying in a hammock or cradle: rocking and swinging movements stimulates the sense of balance and the brain's development. If the child is embraced, for example in a carrying sling, its breathing and heart rhythm will be stimulated and anti-stress hormones will be released in the baby's body. The carrying positions should be varied.

— Letting the child lie in a sack-chair or on a beanbag cushion gives the feeling of being embraced and for stimulation of the sense of touch.

— Avoiding use of a babywalker, bouncing swing, as well as extended use of a car seat or baby recliner.

The older child

— Giving the slightly older premature child infant massage.

— Letting the child play with, and in, water stimulates several senses, in particular the sense of touch.

— Giving the child the chance to swing, crawl, hop, run, and play on the floor develop the balance and gross-motor senses.

— Letting the child lie on its front over a kangaroo ball (big bouncy ball) while it is swung or swings up and down by itself and makes rhythmic noises—perhaps just a few words, repeated rhythmically—strengthens the senses of balance and touch, and the rhythm is the introduction to language understanding and speech. The rhythmic movements in combination with rhythmic sounds are good speech training.

— Letting the child play in a hammock—though one must be careful not to let the game become too vigorous or to continue for an extended period. A physiotherapist or an occupational therapist will be able to recommend good SI exercises for use in the hammock.

— Letting the child play on a skateboard, preferably following instructions by a therapist, enables the child to experience heaviness, improves the body's stability, fingers, arms and body are strengthened, and the child's body image is intensified (Tóroddsdóttir, 2001).

— Playing in the countryside where the child can move to its own rhythm has a positive and calming influence on the mind, and the chance to move at its own pace is important for the rhythm and harmony of the child's body.

— Giving the child physical chances to blossom in the daily routine so it can develop and strengthen motor skills and all the senses.

— Letting older children stand on one leg, playing hopscotch, climbing, hopping down, balancing along a wide line or a thick rope, and catching a big ball with both hands develop the gross motor skills, the coordination of the senses, and balance. The ball should bounce from the floor to begin with; later this can be expanded to include all types of ball games.

— Letting the child draw and paint as well as playing with Lego or similar toys where the fingers are very involved develops the fine motor skills. Strings, branches, twigs, pebbles and sea-shells are good natural materials that give the child a sensory good experience at the same time as strengthening the fine motor skills.

— Letting the child use eating utensils by itself as soon as possible.

— Letting the child develop its mouth musculature by playing with its food, for example, by licking food from the corners of the mouth, by picking up a little pea using the tongue or the lips, or other imaginative ideas that demand the use of the motor skills that involve the mouth.

— Letting the child sit or lie in a sack-chair with a ball blanket.

These suggestions of training and stimulation of the senses and motor skills, and avoidance of overstimulation are *general*: there are many others. A child with delayed motor development and problems in integrating its sensory input should have a training programme tailored to its special needs. The child trains with the therapist, and many educational toys are used. This will normally take place in a training-room, but some premature children will have a requirement of doing exercises at home, in familiar surroundings. This means that the therapist has to be creative in the selection of tools and exercises. As a part of the training programme, the therapist will give the parents and possibly also the nursery teacher or educationist a few simple suggestions that are easily learned, on how to stimulate, and these are incorporated as a game in daily life (Tóroddsdóttir, 2001).

A few Danish Councils have established obligatory sense and motor skill checks for all children when they are 4½ years old; if this is not provided, one can, if sensorimotor problems are indicated, be put into contact with a physiotherapist or occupational therapist through the surgery nurse, day care (in private homes) institution, or the children's day ward at the hospital.

Delayed motor development, language difficulties, and SI problems have a detrimental influence on self-confidence, so motor skills training and SI training cannot stand alone. It is also necessary to work psychologically and educationally with the child, and the method of care has to be adapted to its special needs.

Holding therapy

Eye contact is the most intensive contact between people and the direct route to the central nervous system and the limbic system, which controls emotional development.

N. Møller (2001, p. 8)

Holding is a psychological concept that covers the mother's ability to create an environment that advances the child's development.

Holding therapy is a psychotherapeutic treatment in which the parents are urged to insist on establishing contact with the child in an emotional process where the mother or father holds the child to give it closeness, comfort, and contact. In this situation the parent encompasses the child and its emotions.

Due to the child's resistance against feeling or expressing its own emotions, the parents' insistence on contact will often lead to resistance and rejection by the child. Here it is the therapist's task to support the parents so that they will not feel rejected and will continue to demand contact, keep holding the child in their arms, and insist on eye contact and the right to encompass their child's emotions.

It is through eye contact that attachment is created and strengthened.

The goals of holding therapy are:

— to help the child express repressed emotions and needs;
— to strengthen the contact and attachment between child and parents.

Holding therapy can be beneficial when the preschool child has serious interaction and attachment problems. Problems can be caused in part by the difficulties in interpreting the premature child's feeble signals and thus be able to satisfy the child's needs, and in part by the early separation and consequent feeling of betrayal. The child may react by rejecting the parent by whom it feels betrayed. This can be unreasonably difficult for both parties and for the family as a whole.

Many adoptive children are also born prematurely, though this is not always documented in the papers that follow the child from the relevant country. But as a result there are also many adopted children who react by rejecting one of the parents.

Holding therapy is practised by, for example, psychiatrists, psychologists, or family therapists. The duration of a course of training varies with each individual, but it can stretch over many months. The training can be demanding, but the effect is worth it. A mother of a premature adopted boy of 4 years says: "Here we have Anders before the 6th of December and Anders after the 6th December [the date of the beginning of the holding therapy]. At last we are a family."

Nutritional supplements

If children are to have a chance to cope with the colossal demands made on them, then the fundament—nutrition—must be in order.

F. Bräuner (2003, p. 5)

The weakened immune system, problems with health, and often poor growth of children born much too early demand particularly healthy and nourishing food. The immature brain has a need of energy to growth and development. During the first year, 60% of the child's energy intake is used for the brain's growth. A child who is suffering from an acute illness has a significantly raised energy demands.

There are very many natural food supplements that help to improve appetite, sleep, immune system, that remedy or help coping with respiratory diseases, gastrointestinal problems, ear infections, and so on, that stop infections at the initial stage, lessen the symptoms, and reduce the duration of illness.

Products in liquid form are assimilated more easily by the body.

At some point it may be necessary to provide an extra amount of vitamin A, which is, for example, beneficial to the mucous membranes, and vitamin C, which improves resistance to infections. Both can be obtained or derived from natural sources, for example Total-A and Bio-C or Acerola C-vitamin.

There is good advice and guidance to be found in *A Kid's Herb Book: For Children of All Ages* (Tierra, 2000) and in *Children's Herbal Health* (Tenney, 1997).

Some of the most tested and used products are described below, but there are many more on the market.

For digestive difficulties

A good oil, such as for example, *Eye Q* or *Udos Choice*, can advantageously be added to the food. This oil can be purchased in health shops. It contains a unique combination of plant oils and the important Omega 3–6–9 fatty acids. It does have a strong taste and may be too much for infants, who can instead be given some cold-pressed oil of thistle.

Natural products for establishing a good appetite and a healthy digestion are available in most Western countries (much information and many suggestions for infant and child nutrition are given on www.herbalremedies.com/herremforchi.html).

Many have had good experiences with *Vita Biosa*. The lactic acid bacteria in the product are invaluable for the proper function of the gut. In contrast to most other gut-regulating products, this does not contain milk sugar (lactose).

Diet supplements

If the child has a reduced appetite or none at all, it can be difficult to get it to eat the above mentioned food supplements. As an emergency solution and to break the cycle, one can give the child diet supplements.

The doctor, surgery nurse, and pharmacist can provide guidance in the selection of these preparations.

Fortifying herbs

There are many good fortifying herbs that can be prepared as tea or iced tea with lemon and honey added (before cooling). For example:

— *Fennel* is a bactericide, and it is good for digestive problems, colic, build-up of acid, diarrhoea, and wind in the gut.

— *Aniseed* loosens slime and mucus and is likewise preventative against wind in the intestines.

— *Liquorice root* regulates the blood sugar, inhibits bacterial growth and infections, loosen mucus, and helps to stop cramps.

— *Fenugreek seeds* inhibit bacteria, cleanse, loosen mucus, help to regulate the metabolism, stimulate the digestive function, and strengthen the immune system.

One can always seek advice in health shops or general chemists. The following herb mixtures are particularly recommended:

• *Bio-Strath* is a thoroughly tested Swiss diet supplement produced from yeast, and it contains a long list of herbs. It is produced by a special process whereby the yeast cells are broken down. The product contains 61 different nutritious substances in a natural and easily digestible format. It is free of artificial colouring, preservatives, aromas, gluten, and lactose. It adds important and essential substances to the body, promotes the absorption of the nutritional material from the food, and strengthens the immune system. Elixir or drops can be given in the place of a vitamin pill.

• *Bronchosan* cough drops are a combination of extracts from ivy, thyme, and liquorice root. These plant extracts have a mucus-loosening and hence, a cough-reducing effect. The essential oils act directly on the respiratory system's secretory cells. The millions of cilia that are constantly brushing the mucous surface of the respiratory tract clean of slime and other foreign objects are effectively stimulated, and it is contributory to sorting out imbalances. Bronchosan gives rapid relief in cases of difficulty in breathing and can thus also be beneficial against bronchitis.

Can be taken from 2 years of age. Take daily during periods of coughing.

• *Astra-Vites, Basic Preventive Junior Tabs (chewable), Vita-Kids (improved), Vita-Big-Kids, Mighty Vita Kids* are all products for children (both Astra-Vites and Vita-Kids can be purchased on www.vitaviva.com/en/Shop/Product_Details.3.509.512.aspx, and Mighty Vita Kids, which is available in the United Kingdom, is available on www.worldwideshoppingmall.co.uk/body-soul/ mighty-vita-kids.asp).

• *Echinaforce* contains extract of Coneflower (*Echinacea purpurea*). According to the manufacturer scientific trials, extract of fresh Echinacea purpurea influences the immune system's macrophages (macrophages actively search out foreign bodies) in the body within 15–20 minutes. After this time other parts of the body's complex immune system are activated.

Other products based on fresh Echinacea purpurea—for instance EchinaMild—are also available.

Take as soon as the first symptoms of infection are noticed.

• *Infant Care* is a liquid multivitamin for children in the age group of 1–3 years. Infant Care has been allergy screened, has a high absorption rate in the body and is a clean product without artificial taste enhancers or colouring.

Can be given diluted in water or juice or by the pipette provided. Most children like the taste of natural orange.

• *Kindervital* is a liquid herb/iron elixir that contains vitamins but not minerals; due to the liquid formulation it is easily soluble and is therefore optimally absorbed by the body.

• *Sambucol Active Defence* contains a combination of several immune-system boosters: elderberry, Echinacea purpurea, propolis, zinc, and vitamin C.

Take daily during the autumn and winter as a booster for the immune system and as a preventative preparation. In cases of infection, the daily dose can be increased for a short period.

• *Santasapina Syrup*: This natural, alcohol-free cough mixture mainly contains extract of fresh conifer shoots, and cane sugar, honey, and concentrate of pear. The cough mixture thins the mucus and therefore makes it easier to cough up. This means that the child does not cough as often. Most children like the taste.

Take daily while coughing persists.

- *Urtemix* (previously *"Staaimod"*) consists of elderberries, Echinacea purpurea, Vervain (Verbena officinalis), camomile, liquorice root and aniseed. Each of these individual herbs has positive characteristics and when combined the effect is increased. It is especially effective in cases of middle-ear infection. The product is also claimed to have a beneficial effect on the immune and nervous systems, and also on appetite and digestion. It can be taken as a preventative and immune-system-strengthening supplement (available worldwide at www.naturoghelse.dk).

- *Vita Biosa* is a lactic acid fermented herbal drink that consists of 19 different herbs as well as microorganisms. The special combination and production process inhibits harmful and disease-producing bacteria from developing in the stomach and intestines. This assists in improving the digestive system and in strengthening the immune system. When the gut flora are in balance, the body's general condition improves, and in this manner Vita Biosa can have a beneficial effect against many areas of imbalances in the body.

Take regularly as a preventative and regulation preparation. Can be taken by infants and by persons who are breastfeeding.

Cranio-sacral therapy

After only treatments with cranio-sacral therapy, her energy levels, particularly in the mornings, had improved. The reports from school stated that emotionally she was coping very much better. She was able to give positive accounts of her school day. She coped with going to the recreation centre three days a week . . . which she had not been able to do this school year. . . . Our daughter has had seven sessions and appears to be in a state of equilibrium . . . which we actually have not experienced since she started going to nursery school.

A. Larsen (2001, pp. 11–12)

Cranio-sacral therapy is a treatment method that primarily addresses the central nervous system and the brain. A fluid (*cerebrospinal fluid*) runs through the brain, the spine, the lower spine
(sacrum), and down to the coccyx. The flow of this fluid has a
rhythm of 8–14 beats per minute in adults and 9–16 beats a minute
in children. It is called the body's third rhythm.

Pressure on the cranium can disrupt this rhythm. This can happen, for instance, during vaginal birth, by a fall or a knock on the
head, or from internal pressure on the brain because of alterations
in the blood circulation caused by continuing pain and stress.

The central nervous system and the brain are affected when the
spinal fluid is unbalanced or out of rhythm. A therapist can restore
the rhythm and, by this method, establish a connection between
the right and left hemispheres of the brain.

What can the treatment remedy?

Cranio-sacral therapy can prevent and remedy imbalance. Those
occurring most often in premature children are:

— ADHD;

— hyperactivity;

— learning difficulties;

— colic;

— difficulties with concentration;

— respiratory problems;

— gastrointestinal difficulties;

— problems with motor skills;

— psychic problems, traumas;

— bedwetting;

— spasticity;

— eating problems;

— language difficulties;

— stress and restlessness;

— sleep disturbances;

— sadness.

It should also be mentioned that cranio-sacral therapy can have a beneficial effect on autism and epilepsy.

Treatment consists of light pressure on the cranium, the back, and the sacral region, as well as places where the body has a requirement. The therapist keeps a pressure of 5 g on strategic points and then awaits the body's reaction in the shape of muscle relaxation. It is a most pleasant type of treatment, which most children—including hypersensitive ones—enjoy. The treatment can be used even when the children are very small. Cranio-sacral therapy was developed in 1920 by the American physician Dr William G. Sutherland. Since the beginning of the 1970s, the method of therapy has been developed by another American physician, Dr John E. Upledger, and today it is a branch of therapy practised by specialist doctors in the United States. Many hospitals in, for example, Germany employ osteopathic—working with the bones and the joints—cranio-sacral therapists.

In several American hospitals the therapy is routinely used on all newborn children, as the skull (cranium) is exposed to violent pressure by vaginal birth and this exposes the child to a risk of imbalance of the rhythm in the spinal fluid.

Many parents have very positive experiences with this therapy for their premature children. It must, however, be emphasized that it is important to select the therapist with great care. To find an Upledger CST practitioner in the United Kingdom, contact the Upledger Institute (UK) (www.upledger.co.uk). The International Association of Healthcare Practitioners Directory lists professionals, their telephone numbers, e-mail addresses, and levels of training (copies are available at www.iahp.com; those interested can also refer to articles and other documentation about cranio-sacral therapy at www.upledger .com).

Sandplay

A little sandbox, a lot of figures, and freedom to create one's own universe. There is no need to use words—the inner problems are acted out. Quiet children become more extrovert, aggressive ones discover their gentleness. The zest for life returns.

E. Greger (1999, 16 September)

The background for sandplay is that children develop through play.

Very premature children have had a traumatic start to life. The experience of shock, fear, anger, betrayal, and pain is just as real and intense as it is for older children and adults who are able to express these feelings verbally.

It can be very difficult for most children to cope with traumatic experiences on their own, and the traumas can be the reason why the child is showing poor development in, for instance, the emotional and social areas. Even though the adults close to the child give much care and love, the traumas will remain deep rooted in the child. Dissolving them may require therapy.

The therapist works in a room with a sandbox the size of which encompasses the child's area of vision. The room is filled with toys, and every single piece has its own symbolic value.

The child explores the room's possibilities for play and/or symbols. From the masses of toys it selects that which is the most appealing. For the majority of children a story is acted out inside the frame of the sandbox. The story may show, or reveal a problem; the therapist joins in with this by being there and participating emotionally. At the same time, the therapist keeps sufficient distance to be able to keep a broad overview, so he/she can contribute with suggestions if the child is in doubt.

The child senses the presence, the concentration, the solicitude and, feeling secure in this way, can employ all its sense-potential—it can touch, smell, see, hear, taste, and feel—sense its own self. When the child is aware of itself and its emotions, an opening has been created for the child's own self-regulating and self-healing potential.

Marte Meo therapy

One thing we all do have in common, we develop through inter-action with other people!!!

Therefore it is crucially important that we interact in a manner that promotes development. Today we are aware that the quality of the interaction and the resulting bonding has significance for a child's personality development—that is, the interaction has an influence on whether our infant develops into an active, curious, secure child or an anxious, insecure, helpless child.

J. Wieben (2001, p. 8)

Marte Meo means "by one's own strength". The method is a video-based and solution-orientated form of guidance that builds on the principles for *developmental support communication*.

The method is particularly useful in situations where it is dif-ficult to interpret the signals given by the child, where interaction is not going as smoothly as it should, and also in cases where the child generally has developmental difficulties.

The guidance or advice is based on resources that are already evident in both the child and the adult. The video is used as a working tool. Video recording and analysis of the interaction in normal, everyday situations makes it possible to spot both the child's and the adult carer's initiatives, social competencies, and so on and, based upon this, step by step to set new goals for relevant development in interaction.

The analysis focuses upon the following questions:

— What is the child already is able to do, and what does the recording show the child needs to learn?

— What is the adult carer already doing that is supportive of the child's development?

— Which information does the adult carer need to have to assist the child further in its development? What should be done better, and what needs to be done in a specific manner?

The analysis focuses on elements such as initiative and reaction to interaction. For instance, does the adult wait for the child's initiative? Can she confirm the initiative, and how? Do the adult and child take turns in taking the initiative? (Johansen, 2002).

Information and guidance are passed on to the adult carer with a starting point of selected frozen-frame clips from the video, recordings of the actors' own communication, and with concrete advice on how to act, which can improve interaction and support development.

The Marte Meo method was developed by Maria Aarts, who is from Holland. In Denmark the method has been known and widely used since 1994 in families, in nurseries, kindergartens, day institutions, special institutions, educational centres, nursing homes, and, lately, in schools.

Massage

I consider that the massage has been of great help to me in learning how to handle and play with Mathias and Alexander. It has enabled me to have the same close contact that their mother has when she breastfeeds them. Today they are as strongly bonded with me as they are with her.

Søren (father of Mathias and Alexander)[1]

Giving children massage is a tradition in many cultures all over the world. Newborn premature children are hypersensitive, their skin is extremely thin, and the ability to sense being touched is not fully developed. For this reason, infant massage is too violent for them. However, when they are a little older they can benefit greatly from infant massage, which can:

— stimulate and regulate breathing, blood circulation, and digestion;
— alleviate colic and pain from wind;
— release tension;
— counteract stress;
— expand loving emotional ties;
— strengthen the ability to understand body language.

For those interested in massage for children—parents, surgery nurses, physiotherapists, occupational therapists, reflexologists, and so on—information is available from the International Association of Infant Massage (UK chapter, www.iaim.org.uk/t_training. htm; US chapter, Ventura, CA, www.iaim-us.com). Very sensitive children, such as the prematurely born, are most receptive towards massage at home, in peaceful surroundings. For this reason instructors will make home visits and give individual instructions. Some instructors specialize in the massage of children with special needs (see above-mentioned websites).

NLP therapy

We have been given the world's most advanced computer as a birth present—namely the brain—but we did not get the manual! Through NLP techniques we can learn how to use our brain and our language more effectively.

H. and J. Makani (2002, p. 4)

NLP originally stood for Neuro-Linguistic Programming, but leading Danish NLP experts have opted to rename it Neuro-Linguistic Psychology, which they consider more correct.

Because of the early separation, the imposed pain, and the unpleasant experience, premature children are "programmed" to feel that they are not worth loving. NLP techniques can be contributory to re-programme this self-perception. During the child's treatment, the therapist will make use of supplementary methods such as story telling, drawing or painting therapy, or bodily methods of expression.

NLP therapy often includes time regression, where the therapist, by means of simple techniques, leads the child back to the foetal state, the birth, and the time following birth. Through the child's contact with its early experiences it is enabled to rediscover the condition of security, trust, and closeness that had existed before the trauma arose. Now, armed with its new knowledge, it can get rid of the old emotional ties and get a deeper awareness of causes and circumstances, in this way getting help to create new perception patterns of "I *am* good enough, and I *am* worth loving".

Osteopathy

Osteopathy, also called manual medicine, is a manual method of treatment that aims to examine and treat the human organism holistically. The aim of the treatment is to restore the body's full functionality, and it is based on the thesis that the body's structure and function are mutually interdependent.

The osteopath looks at the way the skeletal bones, joints, connective tissue, muscles, inner organs, and so on, work together and influence each other. By considering the body as a whole and by delving into the deep root causes of the symptoms osteopathic treatment can rapidly achieve effective and lasting results.

The osteopathic techniques include gentle mobilization techniques of joints and muscles and specific manipulations as well as stretching and deep massage of muscles, connective tissue, and tendons. By correcting the body's soft tissue, the osteopath can improve the joint's movement as well as the circulation of the blood. In this way the nourishment and oxygen supply to the tissues is improved at the same time as waste products are removed from the tissues. The treatment can release nerves that have been trapped or squeezed, and the nerves can be ensured a sufficient blood supply. The body is stimulated to regain its normal function.

The osteopath combines medicinal and mechanical with structural methods, both at diagnosis and at treatment. In, for example, German, English, and Australian hospitals, osteopathy is used in combination with cranio-sacral therapy; this combination is also used by a few privately practicing therapists in Denmark. Osteopathic cranio-sacral therapy is an expanded method of treatment that can be effective to help with, for example, colic, gastrointestinal problems, respiratory illnesses, sleeping difficulties, difficulties with concentration, build-up of stress, restlessness in the body, weakened memory and sensory-integration problems. The treatment is a pleasant and relaxing experience for most.

Practical aids and appliances

The first time Mikkel had the ball blanket put over him, he screamed, so it demanded a bit a of getting used to and patience, but after two days he accepted it and I got my first night's sleep for nearly a year—wonderful. When we got the blanket, Mikkel was unable to concentrate, his movement patterns were very hectic, and he had only reached the stage of lying on the floor and rolling about.

During the first week he became calmer, learned to sit up, and was less demanding at night.

At 15 months he was almost at the right developmental stage. He loved a good hugging session and searched out bodily contact himself. He was a happy gentle little chap with lots of courage to tackle life. Last but not least, he had found a normal sleeping pattern.

A. Thorsen, mother of Mikkel, born Week 33[2]

Carrying sling and baby sling

All infants, but particularly premature ones, have a need of a gentle transfer from the womb to independent life. "Attachment parenting" is a concept that is gaining more and more acceptance world-wide. There has been quite a great deal of research done on the topic of attachment parenting, and the results show, among other things, that children who are in the arms of one of the parents for most of the day become more secure and calm, cry less, secrete anti-stress hormones, and have their breathing, their organs, sense of balance, sense of touch, and muscle and joint senses stimulated. The close contact with warmth and nearness is also very conducive to parent–child interaction.

A good carrying sling or a baby sling can make it possible to have the child near the body during most of the day. It is also possible to carry twins in one or two slings (www.betterbabysling .co.uk).

Ball blanket

The ball blanket (www.rompa.com) stimulates the senses and in this way creates an increased body awareness. The blanket is filled with plastic balls, and the many balls stimulate both the sense of touch and muscle and joint-position senses because the weight of loose balls gives individual pressure on the body in a pleasant manner.

If one moves under the blanket—for example, turns over in the bed—the balls roll a bit, and one gets new points of pressure, and consequently new responses are sent to the brain. This increased perception of the body and the body's boundaries calms and gives security. It has a de-stressing and encompassing effect because it helps to inhibit impulses sent to the central nervous system. The stimulation caused by the balls induces tranquillity and increases the child's attention, concentration, and learning skills.

The ball blanket was developed in Denmark based on the theories about integration of the senses by the American psychologist and occupational therapist, A. Jean Ayres. The ball blanket is used for children with many different problems, such as, sensorimotor problems, tactile shyness, ADHD, sleeping difficulties, autism, and spasticity. These children often find it difficult to feel and be aware of their body.

It is a good idea for the adult to try out the ball blanket before letting the child try it. It is important to make the child interested in it, which can be done by first playing with it. The child can, for example, make a cave out of it, run over it, sit with it wrapped around its shoulders, or have it over it while it is read a story.

Next the child can try to sleep under it during the afternoon nap or when there is a need for a brief quiet moment. Once the child is confident about using the ball blanket, it can sleep with it at night.

Experience has shown that when the ball blanket is of assistance, the children love it and will fetch it to sleep under it themselves.

The ball blanket is also made in a baby size. The baby blanket is filled with a mixture of balls and lined with Thinsulate. This gives a secure feeling of being encompassed, and it gives warmth.

Grant for the ball blanket

In some countries the ball blanket is considered both as an aid and as a treatment tool based upon concrete, individual evaluation.

Ball cushion

The ball cushion (www.rompa.com) gives a dynamic sitting position and good training of balance, as the balls are flexible. When one is sitting on the ball cushion, one will move away from the body's centre of gravity—the brain will sense this and give the signal to move the body's weight in order to maintain balance. The muscles are stimulated so one gets the impulse to straighten the spine, which increases the ability to concentrate.

The ball cushion is beneficial if the child is suffering from motor restlessness and/or has difficulties with concentration and learning.

The cushion can be used to help train balance, and in sensorimotor training it is good to use, for example, in the hammock or as extra stimulation by placing it under the feet.

The ball cushion is used, for example, in connection with:

— difficulties with balancing;

— cerebral palsy;

— ADHD;

— hyperactivity;

— learning difficulties;

— concentration problems;

— low muscle tone (tension).

Cradle

A cradle suspended from a single point (e.g., a hook) is different from other cradles in that it can rock in all directions. This is particularly good for premature children because in this manner the development of both the senses and the organs is stimulated—in particular the sense of balance, with a corresponding influence on development of the brain and central nervous systems. Motor skills and language are also given a helping hand by the swinging movement, and the child feels secure in these conditions, which are reminiscent it of the time spent in the womb.

The child can start the cradle swinging by itself and thus gain more awareness of its body.

The Leander cradle (www.leanderform.dk and many other websites) is one of those recognized cradles that are suspended from one point. The mattress that comes with the cradle is filled with organic buckwheat shells, which have good warmth-regulating properties. This is of benefit for the child born too early who, immediately after leaving hospital, still has a need for some help to maintain its temperature.

The cradle can be removed from the suspending hook and moved as desired; this can in particular be of benefit if the premature child prefers to fall asleep in the parents' room, or if the child is going to sleep in a new place and has a need of the security given by the familiar cradle.

The Leander cradle is suitable for allergy and asthma sufferers.

Once the child is old enough to be to sit by itself the cradle can be used as a toy, still with a function of stimulating the senses.

Everyday psychology

Love me most when I least deserve it—because that is when I need it most.

Trine Rosenberg (2002a, p. 24)

Premature children who are sensitive, suffer from low self-esteem, and lack self-confidence have a need in every day life for adults with a high degree of identification of their problems, understanding, care, compassion, and love.

- *Offer care*. The care that the child has been lacking because of the necessary painful and unpleasant treatment, as well as the separation, give the premature child an extra need for care later on.

In order that the basic trust and firm bonding can be established, it is important that in early childhood all the child's basic needs are consistently satisfied as soon as they arise. If in this phase the child cries, it should have immediate attention if one wants to avoid influencing the child's emotional development in a negative direction. There is no reason to fear that the infant is being spoiled so that it will take control. The child has to be a bit older before it is able to play psychological games.

• *Be aware of the importance of encompassing the child's feelings*—including so-called negative ones, like pain, anger, and fear. These feelings will follow a child who as an initiation to life has been met with discomfort, pain, stress, and separation. A child carrying this sort of baggage will often have a low self-esteem and a lack trust, both in itself and in others. This encompasses all the child's feelings, and to repair them one must express that one understands them—for example: "I do understand that you are feeling upset/angry/frightened!" Embrace the child while talking and let it release its anger/sorrow/anxiety in a secure atmosphere. Afterwards, once the child has settled down, one can talk about how things can now be better.

Statements like "you mustn't be upset" and "there is nothing to be angry about" tell the child that is not OK to have these feelings, and this inhibits the feeling of self-esteem.

• *Give the child a secure base*—a stable daily routine, with firm contact with a few adults and with continuity, structure, and stability of the surroundings.

• *Help with understanding and enduring feelings.* The older the child becomes, the more one can discuss the feelings that well up. But it is possible to set words to this even during the child's first year. If the child is helped to understand its feelings, these become easier to bear and to get through. A crying and upset child must have comfort and time to settle down; only then can one reach the child with words. For instance, if the child does not want to go to kindergarten, there is a reason. If, for example, if it says that it does not want to go because the other children are stupid, the adults may answer: "No, the other children are nice!" At this point the dialogue comes to a halt, and the child is left with a feeling of being misunderstood and not living up to the adult's expectations. If the adult had, instead, replied: "Why do you think the other children are stupid?" there is an opening for dialogue, action, and problem solving.

The child has need of support and confirmation when it feels that it has been unfairly treated, which can happen rather often for a premature child with social difficulties.

Very often children are able, with some help from the adults, to express the causes of their so-called negative emotions. It is a help to the child that the adults close to it pay attention to the problem, accept responsibility for it, and help with finding solutions. The fact that the adult helps the child to verbalize the experience can in itself be a huge relief.

Fairy tales are very good as an aid to experiencing feelings. The child can unconsciously relate the terrible things that happen in fairy tales to the difficulties, fears, and traumas in its own world and in the same way find hope, faith, and happiness by registering the defeat of the bad by the good.

Self-confidence and self-esteem are closely linked to criticism and acceptance.

A child who is lacking in trust, self-confidence, and self-esteem needs to experience success. One can help by ensuring that the child is given chances to clear its previous limitations by giving a gentle push when it is ready to advance and by constantly being aware that one is not doing those things for the child that it is capable of doing by itself. In this manner one can support the child in becoming independent and able to master its own problems and its own life.

The child should be praised when it makes progress or does something special. But one should be aware that praise can also have a negative effect: the child can learn not to rely on its own judgement if it becomes dependent on others' judgement of its abilities, and it can sense if there is no genuine appraisal behind the words, if the praise is given just to please the child. If, for example, the child has created a fantasy world, one can participate in it by asking questions and expressing one's delight in the actual project. The child does not need to know that the scenery is lovely or cleverly thought out but will be very satisfied because the adult is involved and thinks that the invented universe is exciting and interesting. By this method the child senses acceptance, participation, and solidarity, and it gets a sensation of being worthy.

The optimal in relation to the development of self-confidence is to totally avoid criticism of the child! To show that it is okay to make mistakes, that it is acceptable and natural that people are different and have differing needs.

It is almost impossible to avoid criticism, but by keeping this goal in sight one can limit criticism a great deal. It is often just a question of turning negative sentences into positive comments—for example: "Don't hold your knife and fork like that—it's really wrong!" can be expressed as "Look, if you hold your knife and fork like this, then it is much easier for you to get the food on the fork."

One can practise positive language, and if one is constantly aware of it, then within a few weeks one can become so adept at it that gradually one unconsciously uses positive phrases.

Some children withdraw into themselves and shut off when they are exposed to stress and other mental pressure. Others are extrovert and can be whiny and/or aggressive. The reasons for the reaction can be precisely the same: the two differing patterns of reaction are related to children's innate nature—they will react to feelings either inwardly or outwardly.

The child reacts from emotions or needs. One meets the child when one focuses on precisely these areas and avoids talking to the head—when one actively listens, makes the effort to participate in the child's world, and speaks from the heart.

It can be difficult if the child is very angry, aggressive, and standoffish, but precisely this behaviour is an expression of the child's powerlessness and frustration, and it shows that the child has a need of loving understanding and for someone to accept responsibility for changing its position for the better.

Children who seem not to react—quiet children—demand a high level of awareness, because they have just as many disappointing and difficult experiences as do those who do show their feelings, but they turn their emotions inward. There they are stored, constantly nagging and laying the foundation for mental problems that will sooner or later—but perhaps not until adulthood—manifest themselves and demand attention.

Children—particularly children with a low self-esteem—have a need to be seen, encompassed, and accepted and to feel attachment. Time alone together with one of the parents is important in this connection, both during the day and, by means of small outings, possibly lasting a few days at a time.

Increased self-confidence and self-esteem help the child to get a feeling of greater security and less fear. When a child feels "good-enough", loved, and competent, it will feel secure in its surroundings and have confidence it its own capabilities. It will be able to master its own life and its own difficulties—it will become an independent, content, well-functioning child.

It can take a special empathy and ability to interpret the child's signals. If one finds this very difficult, it can be useful to note down and describe over a period those situations that provoke the reaction. This may give an outline of the situations that stress or overstimulate the child, and this can, in turn, help to give a clear picture of how little and how much the child can handle.

One can also attempt to find answers to following four questions:

— What does the child experience?

— What does the child feel?

— What does the child need?

— What is the child asking for?

The Marte Meo method is very useful in efforts to interpret the child's signals.

An insecure child has a need to be very close to an adult it trusts when it has to face new experiences. When little by little the child feels secure in the new situation, then the adult can withdraw a bit and let the child realize that the situation can be securely handled by itself. It is, naturally, very individual when the time is right to do this.

A child with reduced ability to function has a need of adults who can help to create an alliance with the child against the problem. Together they can focus on the child's resources, creativity, and imagination. The child is the focal point: the child must solve the problems, but with parents and professionals as allies. The child who has the chance to confide in a professional and to make the decision whether or not to involve the parents may find it easier to be open about some problems that otherwise it may find difficult to talk about.

Possibilities of educational support

> We must acknowledge that children born too early have many needs that we do not cover at present, because we do not know enough about them. Educators must realize that a child's behavioural manner can have a connection with a premature birth. Otherwise we will end up in those situations where educators misunderstand the behaviour and attach some of our modern diagnoses to the kids: "ADHD", "nuts", "hyperactive", and all those terms we use about those children who won't sit quietly when we tell them to.
>
> S. Riise (1996, pp. 4–5)

Premature children who have a reduced level of functionality in one or more areas may need special educational support. Even though the day-care centre offers small, peaceful boundaries, there may still be some things there that are overwhelming for a sensitive and reticent child.

The playroom may be experienced as much too drastic an experience, and then the weekly visit will have to be abandoned, at least for a period of time.

Once the child has gained a better feeling of security and some more courage, it may be able to cope with short periods in the playroom if it arrives before the other children, while there is still peace in the room, and if it sits with the nursery teacher close by the activities. If the day-care teacher can get a colleague to keep an eye on her other charges, she will be able to give more support and attention to the premature child.

Not only the playroom, but also visiting other nursery schools, outings, parties, and other activities that diverge from the daily routine can be too overwhelming for the child. Therefore it ought to be protected from these until it shows that it is prepared for them.

When the premature child is at an institution, this must represent the child's secure base. The child must have total trust in one or more adults in order to feel secure, just as a structured daily routine with a settled rhythm in many cases is an important condition for this security.

Some suggestions as to how one can create a good, secure day for a child who is insecure, sensitive, frightened of new places, new persons, and new places, and/or has problems in collecting the varied sense impressions to a meaningful whole are given below.

— *Preparation for start at the institution.* It can ease the child's first days at the institution if it has previously, under different circumstances, met one or more of the children who attend the institution as well as the head teacher.

— *Plenty of time for the child,* both at home and in the nursery school; extra time to get dressed, to eat, to finish a game, and so on.

— *Plenty of time for leaving* the child at nursery school, so the situation does not become stressed. The child has a need for contact with the teacher before the parent says goodbye and leaves—but not so much time to say goodbye that this is prolonged unnecessarily.

— *The same teacher or helper to receive the child every morning* (as far as possible), and firm rituals and routines from the beginning of the day.

— *Long period of* preparation, so the child has help to cope with the period of separation and to adjust to the new, overwhelming environment.

— *Firm everyday rhythm,* both daily and weekly, so the child always knows what is going to happen. Predictability is a very important factor in the attempts to help the child overview its day.

— *Changing between concentration and free play* gives the child a firm structure and possibilities to find peace and "self-gathering". Alternating between taking in impressions and expressing them gives a good balance.

— *Good interpretation of the child's signals,* whether it expresses these verbally or by body language. If the child is anxious about new things and new experiences, then it must trust and feel secure for it to be prepared for new challenges. A little push can help the child to overcome its fears and in this way experience success, but it is very important that the child is ready. If it is pushed to do something that it still is a long way from being ready to do, it will lose its trust in the adult, feel misunderstood, and will furthermore have a feeling of defeat.

— *Fixed room and same group of children,* and fixed place at table and in the lockers gives predictability and security.

— *Firm educational line,* firm line of direction, clear rules, and consistency give an overview and security. The child needs to have boundaries.

— *Observe, understand, and comply with the child's needs.* For an adult carer for a child with special needs it is more important than normal to put one's own requirements on the back boiler in situations where they can cause conflict with the child's needs. The child's basic security and thus its ability to dare to explore the world are totally dependent upon its needs of being seen, understood, and complied with. It is important to differentiate between desire and needs. To fulfil the child's needs does not mean to pamper it beyond all reason: one of the requirements is to know the social rules and to know that there are clearly defined rules and limits. Some children have a need to decide about clothes, hair, food, toys, and so on in order to feel that they have a certain amount of control. The necessary limits can be enforced in other situations.

— *Clear communication.* A child who has difficulties in integrating sensory impressions will frequently also have difficulties in paying attention. It will find it difficult to keep track of messages or instructions, so it is important to limit these to a minimum and to keep them clear and precise—to give one instruction at a time and to give the child plenty of time to work through the instruction and to reply. The pre-nursery-school child also needs to be told what it should do and when. It is not yet ready to manage its time.

— *Loving and gentle way of talking.* The insecure child who has, since the beginning of its tender life, had so many painful experiences in its contact with other people is very easily startled and frightened if one shouts or scolds. And as the premature child often has a low self-esteem, this will reinforce the experience of not being good enough. Threats must be avoided totally—they have an entirely negative effect.

— *Quiet surroundings and few people near the child.* These are important for an insecure child with difficulties in integrating its sense inputs. That is why a small institute with few children in small groups and well-planned routines is preferable. In private day care the playroom will often be too overwhelming for the child.*

— *Limiting or avoiding excursions* because of the need to maintain a firm rhythm and to avoid overstimulation and provoking fear.

— Limiting or avoidance of substitute day care when the regular carer is unavailable, for the same reasons as mentioned above.

— *Prepare the child thoroughly and in good time* for new things and experiences. The reality must correspond with expectations, which are created by the firm rhythm, the rituals, and the discussion of what is going to happen.

— *Fetching and bringing the child at the same time each day* provides predictability and security. If it is not possible to collect the child at the usual time, it is important to tell the child when it will be collected—though naturally not by use of the clock but, for example, "just after you have had your fruit", or something similar.

Day care

It is beyond the scope of this book to enter into great detail concerning various countries, but for each, the general guidelines outlined in this chapter are relevant. Contact the local social services for details relating to specific countries (relevant information can be found on www.childcarelink.gov.uk/index.asp; www.ncac.gov.au and www.australia.gov.au/9; www.usachildcare .org).

It must, however, be borne in mind that the best solution for the child may be to be kept at home, rather than have to cope with being cared for by a stranger, particularly if the need for a 'visiting' day carer is only for a short period of time.

— Registered childminders look after your child along with other children, usually in their own home.

— They are allowed to care for up to six children under the age of eight, including their own—but only three of them can be aged under five.

— Self-employed, they decide on working hours. Most are willing to work early mornings, evenings and weekends as well as part-time—perfect, say, for school drop off/collection, and holidays.

— All childminders are required to have completed a basic training course, including first aid, and most go on to do further training and professional development.

How can I be sure of good-quality care?

Childminders must be registered and inspected by the Office for Standards in Education (Ofsted), who carry out regular checks on the home and childminder. All adults living and working in the childminder's home will be police- and health-checked. Not all have childcare qualifications. Once you have met and interviewed a childminder, you will get a feel for whether they are suitable for your children. (www .childcarelink.gov.uk/index.asp).

The schoolchild

Very premature children are often less developed in one or more areas, and so it can take special deliberation as regards to the time to start school, as well as selection of the school. Close collaboration between professionals and parents can create a good basis for making the right choice. For the parent it can be comforting to know of the demands the child should be able to fulfil in order to be ready to go to school. With regard to selection of a school, it will be optimal for some children to attend a special school. Others have a need for the smaller conditions and greater creative possibilities for unfolding that the progressive free schools can offer. Rudolf Steiner schools can be a good choice for psychically and emotionally fragile children who have, in addition, need of a high degree of predictability and structure. Some will thrive in a normal state school. Regardless of which school is selected for the premature child, the child needs peace and firm guidelines in the classroom, and for the teachers to have understanding of and take into consideration these special needs. It may be necessary and most beneficial to have a support teacher for the child in the normal school class.

The change from preschool to school can be difficult for a child who retreats from new, unknown things, people, and places. The child can be prepared by repeated visits to the school, possibly initially outside school hours, so the child has the chance to accept and adapt to the new physical circumstances. Following this, the child, together with one of the parents, can visit during school hours.

If the child does not already know some of its new classmates, then one could possibly invite one or more of them home to visit before the school starts.

The child may need a parent to be present for the first few days at school—not necessarily in the classroom, but perhaps in the corridor outside or in the school yard.

Attention difficulties and learning problems become really apparent once the child reaches school age. If the schoolchild with these difficulties has not had any sensory-integration training and motor-skill training, then these should be begun at this time.

At the same time, the child has, in common with the preschool child, a need for structure and predictability, a need of help to remember, understand, and evaluate, a need of clear rules and messages, clear instructions, and clearly defined tasks, which do not have too many solutions. The child may find it difficult to understand and register messages given to the group: it is then necessary to ensure that the message has been received and understood by the child. For the child to able to concentrate, it will need peace and quiet and not too many sense impressions, and will often need help to organize its work.

The difficulties with learning may be caused by the SI problems, but a weakened memory will also make it difficult for the child to learn. If the child cannot remember previous knowledge and experience, then new knowledge cannot be added, and learning cannot take place. A child who has difficulties in learning due to these reasons will need to have the knowledge imparted by several different methods. For example, it can learn the alphabet by looking, listening, singing, rhyming with, drawing, writing, and shaping the letters. This method is actually obligatory in Rudolf Steiner schools. The general age-related levels of self-independence and skills are very often too demanding for prematurely born children. If the demands are matched to the child's level and abilities, then it feels competent and its self-confidence is strengthened.

Involvement teaching

Abraham Maslow's theories on Self-Actualization have been expanded by William Glasser and developed into practical educational treatment methods: the so-called Involvement teaching (Jerlang, Egeberg, Halse, Jonassen, Ringsted, & Wedel-Brandt, 2002; see also www.wglasser.com). The basic thesis for this teaching method is that when children and adults reach a high degree of involvement with each other, the children can be helped towards self-acceptance. The long-term goal is to ensure that the children increase their self-esteem.

The practical application of the teaching is carried out in institutions and at schools by differing formats of meetings held regularly, where focus is on involvement, non-judgemental attitudes from the teachers/educationalists, commitment, responsibility, as well as democratic management of the meetings.

Glasser has described a hermeneutic process (hermeneutic = science of interpretation), which I have presented graphically (see Figure 3.1).

The practical work with the child consists in the educationist's or teacher's daily involvement with the child and in collaboration with colleagues and parents.

The hypothesis is founded on the difficulties that practical work with the child has identified and on detailed discussion with colleagues and the child's parents. Once there is consensus about the hypothesis—which can be amended as the discussions progress—an educational/psychological strategy can be planned, and action can be initiated from this. Following a previously determined period of time, progress, and observations of the child's reactions, a new hypothesis is proposed, and a new strategy is worked out. New hypotheses are postulated, and new strategies are planned and set into action, until the strategy succeeds in affecting the child's condition and behaviour to such an extent that the child achieves harmony with itself and its surroundings. This is the foundation of the child's self-realization and feelings of self-esteem.

An example

Norman is in Class 1 (Year 1). The teachers have noticed that he does not concentrate, finds it difficult to receive and understand messages given to the group, finds it difficult to sit still, has trouble with learning, and has problems with joining in games in a positive manner. He is also reticent towards new tasks and new experiences.

The class teacher investigates Norman's background; through the parents he is given information about Norman's birth and the following sequence of events, his relationship with his family, his home life away from school, his strengths and weaknesses, as well as his pattern of reaction and strategies for coping.

Based on this information, the teacher describes Norman's situation as she perceives it:

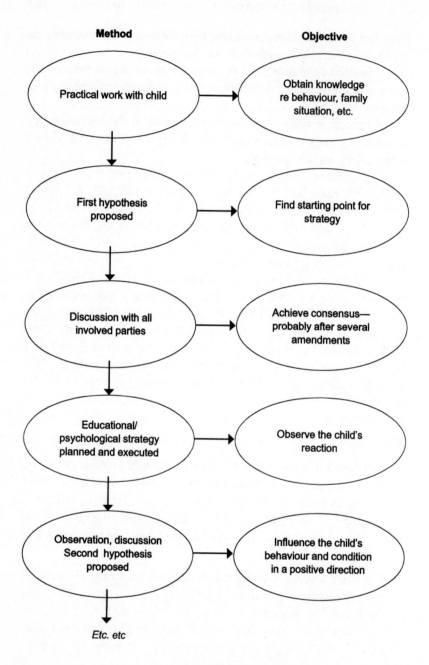

Method

Objective

Practical work with child → Obtain knowledge re behaviour, family situation, etc.

First hypothesis proposed → Find starting point for strategy

Discussion with all involved parties → Achieve consensus—probably after several amendments

Educational/psychological strategy planned and executed → Observe the child's reaction

Observation, discussion Second hypothesis proposed → Influence the child's behaviour and condition in a positive direction

Etc. etc

FIGURE 3.1.   Example of a hermeneutic process:
undefined problem with a child

Due to Norman's extremely early birth he has a memory problems, difficulties with sensory integration, and consequent difficulties with attention. This results in learning and social difficulties. His reduced functionality is lowering his self-esteem and self-confidence, so that he always doubts that he can deal with the tasks given to him, and that is why he is reticent.

The teacher now arranges a meeting with a physiotherapist and child psychologist, and the parents are also asked to participate. The teacher presents his hypothesis, which all accept after a few small amendments. The child psychologist points out that the early experience of fear from the time in the hospital can be a contributory cause of the low self-esteem and the lack of self-confidence. She emphasizes the importance of the parents having a chance to work through their own experiences based on the early birth. The parents relate that Norman very often become aggressive in mid-afternoon. It is decided that Norman should begin a series of sessions with a physiotherapist and that the parent should arrange to have a series of sessions with the psychologist. The teacher is going to create the optimal educational boundaries for Norman as described under "The schoolchild" (see above).

The follow-up meeting is planned for two months later.

The physiotherapist finds during his sessions with Norman that apart from sensory integration problems, he also has low muscular tension and stress build-up in the body, with resulting continual motor restlessness.

The parents are given a training programme to work through with Norman daily, and he is given a ball cushion to sit on at school.

During the two months that the physiotherapist is treating Norman, the teacher notices that Norman sits more quietly, is able to pay attention, and understands much better. He is finding it easier to recognize numbers and letters, and he inverts them less often. He is also better at playing with the other children; he understands the games better and joins in much more positively. His afternoon periods of aggression are lessened, but he still has a lot of internal anger. He is still reticent about trying new things, and he still benefits from a firm educational structured programme.

The parents have become more serene and in harmony. They are better able to tackle and accept Norman's anger. This means that the family interaction has become markedly improved. At the next meeting the teacher, physiotherapist, psychologist, and parents present their observations. It is decided that Norman should continue with the training, but less intensively. The parents' sessions with the psychologist are ended. The teacher continues with the special educational efforts. After a month the parties meet again, and they judge that it is now time to include the child psychologist. She works with Norman's traumas and stress-filled experiences from the time at the hospital and with his feelings of having been betrayed while still a tiny infant. These circumstances influence his self-esteem and self-confidence just as his reduced ability to function has done. The child psychiatrist gives the parents and the teacher some practical advice on how to strengthen Norman's self-esteem and self-confidence.

The teacher routinely observes Norman; at the following meeting she is able to report that he is now a happier, more courageous, better-functioning boy. The parents' experiences are the same.

The special combined effort is completed with an agreement that the teacher and parents continue to observe Norman's behaviour and arrange a subsequent meeting if the need arises.

This educational tool requires many resources, but the effort will be for a limited period, and the extra resources should in all probability give good, lasting results and thus have both a reparative and a preventative effect.

Infant therapy

Hope serves to add warmth to our lives and to light it up.

La Rochefoucauld [1613–80]

Infant therapy is relatively new but not very well known, even though the therapy gives good results. Danish infant therapists are primarily inspired by the French paediatrician, psychiatrist, and psychoanalyst Caroline Eliacheff, author of the book *À corps et à cris. Être psychanalyste avec les touts-petits* [Raging battles: Psychoanalysing small children] (1997), and by Françoise Dolto, author of a book of conversations about children and psychoanalysis (1982).

Method

Traumas are stored even by infants. The organism remembers—an untreated trauma will tie up energy.

The child is given help to handle the chaos in its inner self after a traumatic experience or period. This is done in a caring manner by the therapist in firm, planned therapy sessions, who, together with the mother and/or father,

— makes direct contact with the child;
— recounts the story of its life to the child;
— gives the child hope.

As the chaotic causes are identified, the child is immediately visibly eased; it will quickly begin to function better and better socially.

The therapy sessions are recorded on video and are analysed after the session by the analyst and the parents together.

Therapy is begun with the parents who are helped to identify and confront their own feelings and experiences of the whole period, which has also been traumatic for them. They are also helped to carry the great worry, to release feelings of guilt, and to have hope. All this is the premise for the parents to be able to help their child, so the cornerstone of this form of therapy is the treatment of the parent's crisis. The therapist helps to encompass the parents so that they are able to encompass their child.

• *Phase 1.* Trust is established between therapist and parents. The parents are prompted to meet the child in its regression, give it permission to be little and dependent, give it comfort and security as and when needed and give it room to have desires and games.

• *Phase 2.* The parents are given help to restore the child's trust in the world and to expand its tolerance of frightening experiences in secure situations.

• *Phase 3.* Symbols and words are linked to traumas and emotions. The parents are given help to understand and accept what the child is expressing it its play, following which a spoken process can begin.

From the end of its first year of life verbal explanations and emotional labels of the child's frightening experiences can be used. Words are fitted to the child's own life history.

• *Phase 4.* Psychotherapy with the infant is initiated.

The tangible words that describe what the child has been exposed to are identified and written down. The parents approve the words.

The therapist approaches the child with respect, sensitivity, and empathy, puts tangible words to the child's history, and gives the child hope—hope that the traumas are finished with, that the adults understand, support, and help the child, and that the child can now feel safe and secure.

Those words that the therapist frames for the child are arrived at by the therapist trying to visualize just what it was like to be that child, in that situation, at the stage of development it was at when the traumatic event happened.

By putting words to the actual situation, the child finds peace and hope.

It is very important that the parents, teachers, and therapist all have a common goal and hope. It is this that gives the child hope.

The child is given help to find inner peace in such a way that it can explore its surroundings and begin to play with the parents, who then in turn give the child the possibility to explore the traumas by means of symbols and action.

Reflexology

Mikkel had been given lactulose in his milk at the hospital, and we naturally continued with this when we came home, but even then his digestion came to a halt, and it caused him a lot of anguish. . . . The very first treatment had an effect on Mikkel. To begin with he had treatment twice a week, and this really helped him. Mikkel now had sufficient surplus energy to play and smile at times. . . . It is my considered opinion that reflexology strengthens Mikkel's immune system and has been contributory to the fact that Mikkel has had nothing worse than a slight cold since we were discharged from hospital.

C. Kjærsgaard, Mother of Mikkel, born Week 25[3]

Reflexology can be used for both adults and children of all ages. In connection with premature children it can be obvious to seek out reflexology treatment for the problems that may crop up during infancy. This can be, for example, abdominal pains, long-lasting screaming sessions, constipation, many infections, as well as problems with eating and sleeping.

The therapist massages the body's meridians, which can be affected by means of light pressure on the reflex zones under the feet. The reflex points for those places where the body is in imbalance will be tender or tense. The light application of pressure relaxes these points and, by way of the meridian, helps to balance organs that are not functioning optimally. The body will itself continue the process for at least 24 hours after the treatment.

Reflexology has become an accepted treatment method in Denmark as a result of several extensive physician-controlled investigations, among others *Zoneterapiens virkning på spædbarnskolik* [Reflexology's effect on infantile colic].

One must be aware that reflexology alone cannot always sort out abdominal problems. If the child is given substitute breast milk and is, for example disposed towards allergies, or if it still has an immature gastrointestinal system, it may be necessary to change to a special milk substitute formulated for premature children or allergy-prone children.

NOTES

1. Brochure *Spædbørnsmassage* [Infant massage].
2. "Behandling" (http://praematur.dk).
3. "Forebyggelse og behandling" (http://praematur.dk).

CHAPTER FOUR

Requirements for provision of public support

In addition to the professionally trained staff employed by the councils and counties who are mentioned in the section "Professionals Involved in Family Support", there are some offers of assistance available to the public that may be of value for premature children with delayed handicaps.

This book covers the prematurely born children's *need* for available public help. As support varies from state to state, and as terms and conditions are variable, it is recommended that parents find information locally—for example:

www.nyc.gov/html/doh/html/phc/phc2.shtml (provides details of support available for residents of New York City);

www.neuropsychologycentral.com/interface/content/links/page_material/pediatric/pediatric_links.html (gives access to several very specific links where more information can be found);

www.centrelink.gov.au/internet/internet.nsf/payments/carer_allow_child.htm (provides support and information for families about premature birth and parenting a premature infant);

www.austprem.org.au (gives support and information to Australian parents and caregivers of babies and children born
prematurely);

www.amba.org.au (The Australian Multiple Birth Association
Incorporated).

Children's outpatient clinic

Even though the children as a rule are monitored by the children's
outpatient department during their first year, there are still important
tasks involving the family's General Practitioner. The first being to
gain the parent's trust.

Professor G. Greisen, MD (1994)

In most countries the practice is that families with very prematurely born children are registered, for monitoring purposes, for a
shorter or longer period with the hospital's children's ward after
the child has left the hospital. At these control visits the child is
weighed and measured, its development is evaluated, and food
and nutrition is discussed. The above are the basic areas investigated, but, dependent on the staff, the child's condition, and the
parents' contributions, many other aspects may be discussed at
the control visits.

The paediatrician at the children's outpatient clinic may be the
professional who can certify that the child needs help and that
the family should have contact with other specialists in child care.
The paediatrician may also be the contact who can arrange for special intervention or arrangements to be made and for the granting
of financial support.

For instance, there may be a need for the child to have contact
with an osteopath or an occupational therapist (or physiotherapist)
in order to have an evaluation of sensorimotor development, or for
the family to get help in order to optimize the parent–child interaction, or for a preschool child consultant to advise the family on
those areas where the child has special needs, or that one or more
family members are offered psychological treatment.

It could also concern a grant towards extended maternity/paternity leave; or refund of lost earnings for one or both parents; about getting a funding statement for additional support at day care or in an institution so that the usual adult-to-child ratio is increased, ensuring additional adult presence; or a supportive preschool teacher in the institution. The paediatrician in the outpatient department should be able to help with these with a written statement of the actual requirements.

There might also be a refund of expenses incurred in hiring a breast pump, transport between home and hospital, and possibly special breast milk substitute.

Integrated clinic

We contacted the Integrated Children's Clinic in Copenhagen, and fortunately they took us seriously—something we were unaccustomed to—and Cæcilie started attending for some guidance with language stimulation and language construction with a specially trained instructor, and also a module of developmental games for 4–6-year-old children whose development was generally delayed. It was really useful.

U. Ejlersen, mother of Cæcilie, born Week 29[1]

Prematurely born children of preschool age, and also during the school years, have a need of cross-disciplinary monitoring, and here a common geographical base is desirable. There is a need for a free monitoring service that could be used by all families of preschool children who have developmental difficulties. In addition to parents, all categories of professionals should be able to contact this regarding their worries about a child's development and wellbeing.

The service ought to include a trans-speciality evaluation of the child, a joint plan for psychological, and educational status and eventual treatment required, and, naturally, a detailed plan of how it should be carried out.

If a need for intervention or treatment arises, it should then be possible to establish an ad hoc group to cover this.

In connection with the premature children, the integrated clinic could be of help, for example, if:

— there are problems with interaction between child and parents;
— the child has language difficulties;
— the child has motor-skill and developmental problems;
— the parents need pedagogical advice on how to stimulate a child, even if it is not attending an institution or day care;
— the parents have need of pedagogical and psychological evaluation of the child in connection with, for example, finding help with selecting carers as well possible needs for special education;
— the professionals involved with the child need to cooperate across their various disciplinary areas.

The skills of the following professions are relevant and should be present at, or linked to, the clinic: infant psychologist, child psychologist, children's neuropsychologist, psychologist, speech/ hearing therapist, speech therapist, preschool teacher, occupational therapist, physiotherapist, social carer, osteopath, eye doctor, otolaryngologist, paediatrician, and child neuropsychiatrist.

Any possible serious interaction problems between parents and child should be remedied by the clinic's competencies, possibly by means of Marte Meo method or holding therapy.

Family group conference

Family group conference gives the child a key role. It becomes "visible" in both the investigational phase and the decision phase, and decisions are not made over the head of the child. It is a misconception when we think that we spare the child by not talking about reality. Far from. Imagination is always worse than reality.

A. Grøndahl (2002, p. 27)

If a child has special needs that have not been met for an extended period because they have not been apparent and were therefore difficult to isolate and define, these may create further difficulties for the child and family. If these difficulties are in the psycho-social area, there will be a need for a comprehensive solution—and precisely this is the purpose of the family group conference (Grøndahl, 2002; see also www.frg.org.uk/fgc/FamilyGConference.pdf; www.cyf.govt.nz/1254.htm; www.americanhumane.org).

A family group conference is a meeting in which the family and other important persons close to the family (the extended family) participate, together with the case officer and other involved professionals, such as, for example, preschool teacher, schoolteacher, school psychologist, physician, and nurse. The main point of a family group conference is that it is the family itself who is best qualified to bring forward suggestions on how to solve the problems. The goal is to involve the family and the child and for them to assume responsibility instead of handing it over to the case officer.

The objectives are split into four parts:

1. to give the extended family an increased responsibility when a child in the family has problems;
2. to consider and make use of the extended family's resources;
3. to find solutions that are valid in the long term;
4. to improve interaction between family and social services.

If the child is old enough, it will play a central role in the family group conference, and no decisions will be taken over its head.

A coordinator is specially trained to plan and coordinate the family group conference, together with the family. The coordinator visits and invites those persons the family would like to participate in the family group conference, ensures that all practical things for the meeting are ready, and acts as host for the actual meeting. In addition he/she selects a person from the extended family who is going to act as "advocate" for the child.

As far as possible, the meeting is held in a neutral location, and the family are always involved in selecting this.

A typical family group conference will, on average, take three hours; it is split into three stages:

Stage 1—Information

The extended family participates in the first part of the meeting, as does the coordinator, case officer, and any other professionals who are involved in the child's every day life. Here the family's resources and difficulties are identified.

Stage 2—Family time

The extended family has to get together to find and agree on a suitable solution for the child without participation of the professionals.

Stage 3—Decision and planning

The family present their proposal for a solution to all involved persons as a concrete plan, which has been approved by the rest of the family, including the child, if it is old enough. The case officer approves the plan according to the rules laid down by the law.

There will frequently be a follow-up family group conference where progress is evaluated.

At family group conferences the family can be supported internally by the necessary openness and the objective support given by the professionals to help maintain focus upon the child and its difficulties. The case officer becomes much better acquainted with the family, and in this way misunderstanding between the two parties can be minimized.

The method is often used for families who are lacking in resources and for children who are not sufficiently cared for, but with a little alteration of the definition of the goals it can be particularly suitable for premature children and their families. Not infrequently these families find themselves in a situation where both private persons and professionals involved with them are lacking in knowledge and insight into the conditions that a very premature birth involves, and they may therefore find it difficult to reach and understand the child at its level of development.

The objectives for the premature children and their extended families could, for instance, be:

— to learn and accept the child's pre-history and understand the child's difficulties based on this;

— to set common educational and psychological goals.

The premature child's extended family's resources will often require supplementary input from the various professionals.

If family, close friends, teachers, physician, physiotherapist, case officer, and so on can arrive at a common understanding of the child's difficulties, they have a shared starting point for the setting of common goals.

Combined with the County's usual resources, the family group conference process can also be used as an inspiration to bring a holistic focus to the work with the child and its problems.

The toy library

Jacob goes to the toy library every third month because of his problems with motor skills, particularly his gross motor skills. Connected with the library there is a special preschool teacher, who plays with Jacob for an hour or so and introduces him to different toys. He is allowed to borrow those toys that seem to suit his developmental stage best, to play with at home for three months.

Susanne, mother of Jacob, born Week 32[2]

In Great Britain, The United States and Australia it is possible to borrow or rent educational toys from both free and subscription-based toy libraries. In the United Kingdom this service is, among others, being offered by SEN (Special Educational Needs) departments.

If there is a need for any equipment it will be a good idea to seek specialist advice and check if the equipment can be provided by statutory services.

In several countries it is possible to ask for a community care assessment. An assessor will consider the type and level of need and suggest a range of solutions that may include provision of equipment.

There is no charge for borrowing the toys.

It is the toy library's task to help and support parents of children with special educational needs through lending and guidance in the use of materials that stimulate and aid development.

The child will, through various games, develop the body's movement, use and train all the senses, and collect experience. In addition, it will be exposed to needs for language and to use the language skills it already has.

The toy library is for parents and others who are in daily contact with children with special educational needs.

Cooperation with other professionals can be established, if the parents wish it, so that the toy library's function becomes a natural part of the initiatives that have been taken to help the child.

A few websites as examples:

www.ctl.org.uk (UK);

www.natll.org.uk (UK);

www.scope.org.uk/downloads/factsheets/word/ equipment.doc (UK);

www.cincinnatichildrens.org/visit/facilities/libraries/toy-library (US);

www.bsl.org.au/main.asp?PageId=469 (Australia:);

www.southburnett.org.au/members/community/netl/index. shtml (Australia).

Public care arrangements

Many of the children are hyperactive, their sleeping rhythm was broken at the hospital, and many have eating problems. If the staff at the day-care centre do not know the background or have time to tackle the children's special difficulties, then these children are really at a disadvantage. Then some of them will end up in full-time institutions.

Social advisor Susanne Svenningsen (1996, pp. 4–5)

Apart from the traditional possibilities such as day care, crèche, kindergarten, nursery school, and integrated institution, there might be some alternatives.

In most Danish councils it is possible to become a day-carer for one's own child/children, which can be a clear advantage where there is talk about multiple births. Twins, who each in terms of support count as two children, can represent the entire day-care number of children allowed, and so, naturally, will prematurely born triplets.

Some Danish Councils allow special or basic day care for children with special needs.

Finally, there is a possibility of employing a young girl as *au pair*. Before one decides to follow this option, it can be of benefit to talk with some parents who have tried it. It is possible to find descriptions of people's experiences with *au pairs* on the Internet's various pages dealing with family and child focus.

What should one chose, and at what point?

Just about all recent research shows that children generally gain most advantage by being looked after outside the home, including long-term, and also from when they are less than 3 years old.

This, however, is based upon the presumption that there is a certain quality in the care, and with the adult's interaction with the children being the main criteria for success (Schaffer, 1990). However, the majority of prematurely born children have a requirement for being cared for at home for a longer period—often 2–3 years—not only because of their weakened immune system, but to an equal extent, because of the insecurity and difficulties with attachment that are often present. For the same reasons premature children can have a need to attend the day-care centre for six months to a full year longer than usual.

It can be difficult to decide when the child should first go into day care, and it is equally difficult to judge which offer of care should be accepted. Once the maternity leave is over, it is very frequently the case that parents of a prematurely born child are clearly aware that their child is not yet ready to attend day-nursery care, but the social services judge differently and it is therefore not possible to be granted additional maternity/compassionate leave. Some families find their own solution to this problem, but it does demand a very good income.

If there is doubt about the child's level of development, a broad-spectrum test system can provide help with evaluation and description.

In Denmark paediatricians recommend day care in private homes rather than in a crèche because the lower chance of transmission of infections. Private day care has the additional benefit that there are fewer children, only one adult to have to understand and to form an attachment with, more tranquillity, and a better chance of rhythm, firm routines, and predictability—that is, a better chance of avoiding overstimulation and of creating confidence and good, close social contacts.

Crèches and kindergartens employ trained children's teachers, and they have the possibility to allocate a supporting teacher as well as stimulating and educational toys and tools. But often the child will have a greater requirement for tranquillity and only a few persons to relate to, and a good, well-functioning collaboration between day-carer and nursery teacher makes it possible to offer the necessary educational effort in day care as well.

If there is a possibility of the child getting a funding statement stating that the adult-to-child ratio should be increased, then this can help to give the optimal conditions for meeting the child's special needs. It should be possible to establish trans-disciplinary cooperation via day care and institution, involving, for instance, physiotherapist or occupational therapist, surgery nurse, the centre for supporting materials, psychiatrist, and special needs teacher.

Evaluation

Some prematurely born children will have a need for a supporting teacher, others for a special institute. The methods for sorting out what is needed and what is available can differ considerably, and the individual child's life before starting at an institute can, naturally, vary considerably. Consultants specializing in children can, before the child starts at an institution, evaluate the child's requirements. A broad-spectrum developmental description can provide a good picture of the child's development in the social and emotional areas, play, language development, cognitive development, gross- and fine-motor-development skills, awareness of its body, and awareness of its surroundings.

Many places in Denmark use children's therapists to gauge the children's level of development and requirements. Therapists may work with the special children's educational team, in cooperation with the Council, in private practice, or be employed by the hospital's children's department.

In other places the support team includes "flyers"—personnel who have the task of moving to the various institutions for quick help to children with difficulties.

A special effort does not necessarily require a children's support teacher, specially trained staff, or a special institution—it can also be a special action plan for the child attending a normal institution.

A special educational offer may also consist of an examination of the child's perceptual and motor-skill development. Such an evaluation will be carried out by a specially trained physiotherapist or occupational therapist, in close collaboration with the parents and the child's other care persons.

As a rule, it will be necessary to combine several specialities to obtain a collective and satisfactory evaluation of the child.

Communication and collaboration

Day-carers and preschool teachers have an advantage if they have been informed about the child's history and its eventual special needs. With this information they will be able to accept the child as it is and create the space and special requirements it needs.

The information will also be of advantage if it should happen that no sign of delayed development or special needs are evident at the start of day care. Many effects can become evident only later, which is why continuing attention and extended monitoring is recommended—(see research conducted at Aalborg hospital below).

It can be of major benefit if the surgery nurse passes on her knowledge of the child to the day-carer/crèche, and if staff there in turn then pass on their insight to the nursery school.

There will be a need for open and frequent communication between staff and parents, in step with the child's continuing development. It is very important that all have a common understanding and perception of the child and work together towards common goals.

Social legislation*

I didn't know that parents of prematurely born children can have compensation for lost income. It was quite by chance that I heard about it. It has been absolutely typical that I had to find all the information by myself. It would be an idea to ensure that parents of children born too early are given the information that is needed so that the time at home after leaving hospital does not become totally impossible.

J. Nielsen (1996, pp. 4–5)

The support arrangements for the premature child are often dependent on the economic support possibilities that are permitted by law. These arrangements differ widely in various countries, and it is not within the scope of this book to go into details, particularly as legislation is continuously changing. Examples of links to relevant sites are given in the section on websites at the end of the chapter, the focus being on English-language (UK, US, and Australian) sites. If these do not provide the required information for the individual child's needs, they may act as a pointer for finding further information.

The United States, unlike the United Kingdom, relies heavily on private healthcare. However, support varies from state to state, and as terms and conditions are variable, parents are recommended to find information locally.

Danish social legislation is extensive, and included here are examples of tried and tested methods of support that can be recommended.

The social legislation concerns *children with special needs*, but this concept can be interpreted in several different ways. The conditions for cover of additional expenses are slanted very much towards diagnosed hardships/handicaps.

Prematurely born children can easily end up in a difficult situation because they are often not diagnosed and therefore are in a

---

*Co-author: Social consultant, family therapist Mette Andreassen.

"grey zone". They may have a reduced ability to function, perhaps due to difficulties with sensory integration, difficulties with concentration, and marked, basic fear, but these symptoms can be hard to document and thus it may be difficult find possibilities for help within the rules and regulations.

The family as a whole may have need for extra support, such as extended time off work or practical help in the home, as it can be exceptionally demanding and burdensome to supply a premature child's special needs. It can be difficult to find legal paragraphs, which concern the whole family's situation.

Additional expenditure

Families with a handicapped child (a child with reduced functionality) should by law be financially equal to other families. There should, for example, be the possibility to have additional expenses that occur as a result of the child's handicap/illness refunded.

In order to have the necessary additional expenses refunded it is also a condition that these are above a minimum sum—a level that is regulated annually.

Which additional expenditure should be refundable?

A decision covering additional expenditure requires that an individual consideration should be made. Some additional expenses—for instance, treatment (sensorimotor training, physiotherapy, and so on), tools for treatment, and other aids—will be included in different legislation.

- *Some examples of additional expenditure*
  - food and dietary supplements;
  - medicines;
  - hospital stays (parents spending the night if the hospital does not supply free beds and if it is necessary that one or both parents are present);
  - food and transport expenditure for one or both parents during the child's hospital stay;

— transport for check-up visits and/or treatment;

— hire of breast pump;

— payment for participation in specially arranged courses that concern the child's handicap or illness;

— child care for the child and/or siblings at hospitalization, participation in meetings, treatment, and so on, as long as the child's need for care is a direct consequence of the child's illness and therefore a situation one would not otherwise have been in; supplement towards the expenditure incurred in hiring a nurse/nanny may be obtainable.

- *Compensation for lost earnings*

The very premature child will often have a need to be cared for at home for a longer period due to insecurity, anxiety, fear of separation, poor and unstable sleeping patterns, problems with eating, and so on. It can be difficult to get professional diagnosis in these undiagnosed grey areas, and it can therefore be correspondingly difficult to obtain the required help and support.

Compensation for lost earnings should be available for single days (for example, to cover check-up visits and treatment) as well as for longer continuous periods.

It should also be possible to receive compensation to cover lost earnings at the child's admission to hospital if the hospitalization requires the presence of one or both parents.

- *Support for children and youngsters with special needs*

Many families of premature children have a need for family guidance or similar arrangements where the whole family is involved. The object is to give the family a better interaction pattern and improved internal relationships. It should be possible to obtain economic support in connection with this.

There may also be a need for respite care for the family by letting the child stay with an approved care family, preferably a family that is known to the child and its family. The period of stay is recommended to be a couple of days, typically at weekends and during holiday periods.

The child and/or the family may have a need for a personal advisor or a designated personal contact.

If at all possible, placing the child outside the family home should be avoided.

When there is a suspicion that the child requires special support, the Council should ensure that the child's circumstances are examined more closely. This may involve children with physical, mental and/or social problems.

An investigation should to be initiated in collaboration with the parents and knowledge about the child should be collected, for example, from the child's place of day care, health visitor, or others who have a knowledge of the child's condition.

It is of advantage to all parties if such an investigation is focused on the family's own resources and on those conditions within the family that can contribute to alleviating the difficulties.

- *Support or relief*
  Apart from the possibility of getting supplements towards private care, there may be a case for support or relief for parents or other close relatives who take care of a child with reduced functionality.

- *Practical help in the home*
  In some cases—especially if nursing and care of the child makes it impossible to carry out other duties—there will be, as an alternative or supplement to the compensation for lost earnings, a need for practical help in the home, to release the parents from practical and domestic tasks and free them, instead, to concentrate on the child's needs.

- *Special institutes*
  In those cases where the Council's day-care offers are not suitable for the child's special needs, there may be a requirement for a special institution.

- *Advice and guidance*
  Parents with children or youngsters, or others who actually care for a child, may have a need for family-orientated advice. It should be possible to receive advice anonymously by personal or telephone application.

- *The Danish case—tried and tested social support*

In Denmark most hospitals are allocated a social adviser who can give advice and guidance about possibilities and entitlements and can help with formulating an application to the Council.

Danish social legislation is constructed as a framework, which means that most of the rules do not specify precisely when one may be able to get support or what one is entitled to: the public case officer in each case has to carry out an individual estimate and evaluation. The Council's knowledge of handicapped children and children with special needs varies, and the various Councils interpret the laws in different ways—which in reality means that there may be great differences in the amount of help one is granted by the various Councils, even in the case of families with very comparable needs.

When one applies for help in Denmark, the Council will often request a statement from persons who have knowledge of the child's situation, including the family doctor, hospital, and so on. Collection of these statements will only be done with the permission of the parents. The parents have at the same time a duty to participate by providing the necessary information. When the Council receives a request for help, a "Case" is recorded, and as a parent one is part of the case, which also means that one has the right to request access to the documents, just as one has the right to discuss the information that forms the basis of the handling of the application.

In Denmark the prerequisite for covering of additional expenditure is that *"The child or the young person has a significant and permanent reduced functionality"* or a *"radical chronic or lengthy illness"*. Furthermore, the additional expenditure must be *"essential and be a result of the reduced functionality"*.

The decision thus gives a chance to get a refund of the additional expenditure the family has incurred because the child has a reduced functionality or long-lasting illness. The family must themselves cover that part of the expenditure that they would normally have had to cover.

That it must be "lengthy illness" does not mean that it has to be an incurable illness or handicap. The families of prematurely born children may therefore be included in the target group, as the family are especially burdened for a shorter or longer period. But inclusion is very hit-or-miss.

The fact that a child is born too early is not in itself sufficient to get help. Many conditions are incorporated in the evaluation, including how premature the child was, whether there were complications during and close to the birth, other difficulties, which necessitate especial consideration, and so on. One of the purposes of the legislation is to prevent the child's reduced functionality or extended illness becoming worse or resulting in other, more serious consequences.

In Denmark the legislation covering refunds or supplementary help toward refunds of additional expenditure enables the families of premature children to obtain compensation for lost earnings. It is naturally a requirement that this concerns cases where the loss of earnings is as a natural consequence of the child's reduced functionality or illness, which requires that the child be cared for at home. The best solution is often that one of the parents, or another carefully selected family member, takes care of the child. This can be the case for too-early born children, who due to their reduced immune system or significant risk of illness cannot attend day care.

In Denmark the amount of recompense for lost earnings is based on the most recent earnings, against which are calculated those expenses not incurred by being at home (expenditure in travelling to and from work and the cost of day care for the child).

- *Support for the child in day care*
Prematurely born children very often have need of a funding statement requesting an increased adult-to-child ratio in day care, which means that the day-carers have extra time and the possibility to cover the child's special needs.

For children in kindergarten or school there may be a need to have a supporting person or supporting children's teacher allocated. An application for allowance of extra support hours will in Denmark often be considered based on an evaluation and submission from a health visitor, day-carer, hospital, and so on.

The possibilities for grant allocation and the amount of support hours do, however, vary considerably from council to council.

In Denmark the councils offer free advice and, furthermore, have the possibility of drawing on specialist knowledge (consultancy help) from the County. One can therefore always contact a Council case officer who will be able to give advice regarding support possibilities as well as refer to the relevant instances that fall outside the Danish social legislation.

Social legislation websites

UK sources of information:

www.childcarelink.gov.uk   [*national and local childcare information*]

www.cafamily.org.uk/employment.html   [*about working and caring for a disabled child*]

www.cafamily.org.uk//whenyourchild.html   [*links to Social Services, benefits, childcare, etc.*]

www.direct.gov.uk/Bfsl1/BenefitsAndFinancialSupport/Caring_for_someone/fs/en   [*information about benefits*]

US sources of information:

www.marchofdimes.com/prematurity/5422.asp   [*US link, March of Dimes, gives breakdown of expenses incurred by birth of premature child— not in great detail*]

www.ssa.gov/pubs/10026.html   [*US link, to information about benefits for children with disabilities*]

www.neuropsychologycentral.com/interface/content/links/page_material/pediatric/pediatric_links.html   [*US link, gives access to several very specific links where the more information can be found*]

www.nyc.gov/html/doh/html/phc/phc2.shtml [*provides details of support available for residents of New York City*]

Australian sources of information:

www.centrelink.gov.au/internet/internet.nsf/payments/carer_allow_child.htm;

www.austprem.org.au   [*provides support and information for families about premature birth and parenting a premature infant*]

www.amba.org.au   [*Australian Multiple Birth Association*]

Health visitor

If only we had known the things we know now when we came home with the child after leaving the hospital. Then everything would have been so much easier.

The Mother's Help's first group of premature mothers (1996, pp. 4–5)

When the child is discharged from the neonatal department, the surgery nurse takes over. This can be a major change for the parents, because at the hospital there is so much professional expertise to be drawn upon, day and night.

The surgery nurse has a broad range of skills and can therefore not be expected to be an expert in all of them. This may mean that one can be allocated a health visitor who does not have much knowledge about premature children; but if this is case, one would expect her to increase her knowledge about the topic while the family is on her visiting list.

In more and more places in Denmark matters are organized so that one or more health visitors become specialists in premature children. This is naturally only possible in the larger Counties, which employ many health visitors.

According to Danish law the public health department must offer support to children and families of children with special needs to the full extent and while it is needed. This means that a family with premature children can always contact the health visitor if any difficulties of whatever shape or form arise—even if she is no longer visiting the family home.

The health visitor knows the family, and she knows the public system. She can therefore be a good contact who can observe and understand the family's situation and guide them in the right direction, where care, support from other professionals, possibility of and granting of extra maternal/compassionate leave, and so on, are concerned.

The health visitor and the paediatrician in the children's out-patient department can, in some cases, offer the same sort of help. This can be, for example, to arrange contact with an occupational therapist or a physiotherapist, a psychologist, or other specialists.

In some places the health visitors organize mothers' groups especially for mothers of premature children, but in sparsely populated areas it can be difficult to find a base for these groups. Where this is the case, the invitation can be to participate in a general mothers' group that includes children born at the same time as the premature child's term. In these groups there will naturally not be a background focusing on premature birth and possible consequences of this, so more frequent visits by the health visitor as well as contact (for example, through a society for parents of premature children) can be of benefit.

NOTES

1. "Behandling" (http://praematur.dk).
2. "Behandling" (http://praematur.dk).

CHAPTER FIVE

Professionals involved in family support

Working out an action plan for the child together with the parents, thus ensuring a gathering of all the facts, has great value. And it gives a far better quality and effectiveness to systematize the relevant records.

Hanne Agerholm (2003), leading physiotherapist

A family with a premature child—or more—can come into contact with many professionals through the years. It is relatively recent that there is focus on the premature children's less visible latent handicaps, the topic is not yet a standard part of the syllabus in the relevant educational courses, and post-training courses in the field are limited. There are still quite a few professionals who do not have an in-depth knowledge of premature children and their hidden handicaps. But there is an increasing interest in and awareness of the topic, and more and more is written about it, particularly in medical and nursing publications.

Insight, understanding, empathy, and trust are important traits in those professionals and specialists who wish to help premature children and their families. But it is also extraordinarily important to be aware of the need for cross-specialization and cooperation between

— paediatrician;

— neonatal nurse;

— general practitioner;

— medical specialists (possibly);

— psychologist;

— children's psychiatrist;

— psychotherapist;

— child neurologist;

— child neuropsychologist;

— health visitor;

— physio- or occupational therapist;

— day-school carer;

— educationalist;

— supporting educationalist (possibly);

— teacher;

— special needs teacher;

— social advisor.

In many cases the families have need of a coordinator, because it is extraordinarily difficult in terms of resources to coordinate all contacts with social and health departments at the same time as having to look after one or more children who demand an extraordinary input almost 24 hours a day.

So many families of premature children find it exceedingly difficult to obtain the necessary help and support because in the majority of cases there is no clinical diagnosis on the child. A weakened immune system as well as asthmatic bronchitis, and so on, can in many locations result in extended parental leave—maternity leave—and getting a funding statement for additional support at day care or institution.

But those children suffering from psychological, social, and sensorimotor problems often find it very difficult to obtain this sort of support. In most locations it is rather difficult to obtain professional documentation in this field, and it is still the case in most Danish counties that it is this documentation that releases the concessions.

Psychosocial, sense, and motor skills and other developmental difficulties can be identified with the use of Kuno Beller's description of development of infants (Weltzer, 1993). It can function as documentation of the child's special needs if medicinal evaluations do not cover the relevant areas.

However, a cross-speciality examination of a child with difficulties is the optimal solution. Collaboration between medical, psychological, pedagogical, and physiotherapy or occupational therapy expertise, together with the parents and the child itself, will be able to decide upon the child's development, its personality, its weak and strong sides, and its limitations.

Cooperation between parents and professionals

The professionals' collaboration with the parents requires insight, understanding, empathy, and support, and attention to and trust in the parents' competence. Many parents of premature children are suspected or directly accused of being hysterical and over-protective. Of course it happens that parents who have been very close to losing their child several times and who have lived for years with the uncertainty of their child being handicapped are extra aware and involved. It is very often the case that the child is showing genuine aberrations that do require special evaluation and intervention. Many parents of premature children fight a long, tough battle to give their child as much self-esteem and self-confidence as possible, so that it becomes more secure and independent. This battle is being fought while they have to continually explain and defend their arrangements and actions to people. The collaboration between parents and day-carers/educationalist/teachers is extremely important. These professionals are together with the child for many hours every day and have the possibility to make an impression on the child and to carry out detailed observations.

When the child has to begin at an institution, it is of benefit for all parties involved to make time to have a thorough discussion about the child and its needs. A link in the collaboration is also thorough information to the parents about the institute's activities. This enables the parents to prepare the child in good time for any changes in routines and in general to take precautions in good time when, for example, an excursion, the absence of the main educator, or changes involving the children's groups are about to happen.

Openness and understanding of the parents' heavy responsibilities in the parental role is a significant aspect of the collaboration between parents and educational staff. Parents often have deep-seated traumas in connection with the child's dramatic and premature birth as well as the subsequent period of intensive treatment, during which they have in many cases been close to losing their child.

It is important to remember to focus on the child's abilities, resources, progresses, little quirks, and other positive sides in all collaboration about a prematurely born child. The child should be regarded as a competent individual with a only a few functional difficulties that need work and effort to correct.

If the parents can obtain qualified professional assistance, they will get access to tools that can, in combination with their own skills, create a good unit in understanding the child and anticipate its needs.

Conversely, the parents can contribute to the professionals' deeper knowledge of the child and thus increase understanding and extend the treatment possibilities.

It may happen that the professionals have to make the parents aware that their child has a greater or smaller handicap or dysfunction. This can be difficult and painful for the parents to acknowledge, but it is necessary to accept reality. Only if the child's difficulties and the causes are identified is it possible to implement supportive intervention.

CHAPTER SIX

Parents and siblings

Parents

We must take parents seriously. They have often noticed things about their children that we cannot detect in an examination.

Hanne Agerholm (2003)

Parents of prematurely born children have as disadvantaged an introduction to the parental role as the children have had a disturbed start to life. A very premature birth is a shock. The shock is just the first phase of the crisis situation into which the parents are often plunged. It does not always follow the classic pattern of shock: reaction, acceptance, assimilation, action. It can be chaotic, and the shock can be so paralysing that a reaction only appears months later. The many chaotic emotions that overwhelm one will often be fear, emptiness, powerlessness, guilt, shame, anger, compassion, love, frustration, gratitude, hope, and sorrow. One loses self-control, and the normal, self-assured way of life: action and competence; one is on bare ground in no-man's-land.

The original meaning of the word "crisis" was development, but in the case of premature birth, development can be a very hard road to follow.

The shock is caused by the sudden, and often very acute, birth experience for which the parents were not prepared, by confrontation with a child who does not come up to expectations, and, finally, by the knowledge of the relatively high risk of losing the child, or that it may become handicapped in consequence of the intensive treatment.

Just as there is a reason why the foetus should stay in the womb for nine months, so there is a reason why the woman must carry the foetus for this same period. During this time she matures mentally, emotionally, and hormonally in order to be ready for her role as mother, and the father goes through a maturing period in tune with the woman's expanding abdomen and the child's movements becoming visible. During the final part of the pregnancy it is absolutely natural to arrange the nursery, buy the layette, get a pram, and, where the mother is concerned, to stop work and almost totally concentrate on the approaching event. All these activities make it quite clear that a child is expected, and are thus part of the parents' maturing process (Bowlby, 1996).

Parents of premature children are not able to go through this process. They are caught unawares, totally unprepared.

The second phase of pregnancy, from the 20th to the 29th week, is when the first stirrings of life are felt; the pregnancy becomes concrete, and the expectant woman experiences a mental change towards the maternal function. Only in the third phase, which begins at the start of Week 29, does the expectant mother seriously begin to think about the birth and the consequent separation from her child.

The mother's maturing process involves very clear images of the expected child, culminating in the 7th month. From then on, the clearly perceived image of the child gradually becomes more diffuse as time moves towards term—this is nature's way of preventing too great a difference between expectation and reality. But at a premature birth the pregnancy has only just become actual in the mother's consciousness, the separation process has not yet been visualized and thought about, and the mental image of the expected child is very clear. Consequently, the shock of the birth and the very different-looking child is great. This can be difficult for outsiders to understand, but the parents actually have to go through a mourning process as they lose or abandon their thoughts about the full-born, healthy baby and learn to accept and love the actual child.

The mother has to abandon her expectations of being a good mother who is able to protect her child against hunger, illness, pain, and discomfort. Instead, she has to find new perspectives in the mother role, such as the importance of her close presence, responsibility for the child by means of active involvement in care and treatment, and adaptation to the child's extended need to be encompassed.

A woman who gives birth very early by Caesarean section has no contact with her newborn for the first few hours after the birth, and she does not experience all those things she had hoped for and expected to happen:

> The researchers Klaus & Kennell describe a mother who picks up her child immediately after it is born, and begins to let her fingertips glide over its face. This makes the infant settle down. Soon she progresses to touch the baby's head and body with her palm of her hand, and after five-six minutes she puts it to her breast. The baby reacts by licking the nipple for a long time. The researchers noted that immediately after the birth the mothers were in a state of ecstasy . . . if the mother has the chance during the following days she will probably spend many hours just looking at her new child, pressing it close and learning to know it. [Bowlby, 1988]

Not being able to participate in this experience can be a great loss. The mother of a premature child also loses out on the attention and care that she had only just begun to experience—or maybe not yet—in her role as a mother-to-be. Generally, it is a single traumatic event that is the cause of a subsequent crisis. With a very premature birth it is not only the initial shock of a birth that can be described as crisis-provoking, but also repeated shocks and frightening and anxiety-ridden experiences resulting from sudden difficulties during the course of treatment and from extended, continual fear at losing the child, or that it will be handicapped. These conditions may considerably increase and delay the assimilation process: as soon as one traumatic experience is past and partly worked through, a new one turns up. This can go on for years as, right up to school age, new difficulties can show themselves if they are not prevented early on.

The separation after birth can be very painful for the mother who may later on begin to feel guilt, but it is important to establish that the mother has not done anything wrong—it is not her fault. The critical situation and the routines in most neonatal departments enforce a separation. One can point out that these routines can be, and should be, changed so that there always is a possibility for ensuring that mother and child can remain together immediately after the birth and during the child's entire stay at hospital. That conditions in most places are not yet so must be ascribed to the fact that it is only during the last few years that we have become aware of the crucial significance of early mother–child contact. It can take several years before research projects have uncovered and described these requirements and thus given the politicians a basis for permitting the funding required.

Certain research results indicate that early mother–child separation does not have long-term influence on the mother's involvement with the child, nor on her self-confidence as mother (Schaffer, 1990). Frequently she will be much more aware of her child than mothers are as a general rule. But the child can, as a consequence of the early separation, suffer from mental and emotional problems that will influence the mother–child relationship.

The small positive steps forward in the child's condition, the discharge from hospital, the broader dialog with the child, and the closer bonding all combine to repair the traumatic experiences. But this healing process often becomes disturbed by new difficulties with the child (eating and sleep problems, and so on), difficulties with interacting, unrealized expectations, incredible exhaustion, and a lack of understanding from people. It is therefore extremely important that the family should be closely monitored and supported by the surgery nurse and by the staff at the children's outpatient clinic. The first few months after the baby leaves the hospital it is essential that this is done to ensure the family cope well and do not end up in a downward spiral.

As parents of a premature child with many special needs, one often places one's own needs—including the absolutely basic ones—on the back burner. Despite doing this it is easy to feel as though one is not coping quite well enough: the child may still find it difficult to eat, sleep, and so on. One does need to be told that one is doing a gigantic piece of work, and one needs professional help to track down and anticipate the child's special needs.

There may be great differences in the mental development of, respectively, the mother and the father of the premature child. This is naturally gender-related, but things such as personal history, mutual relationship, age, and social condition play a part.

The mother's care, involvement, and worry may be complemented by the father's control, ability to take a broader view, and optimism, and in this way the parents can be mutually supportive and still support the child in their difficult situation.

The parents of the premature child may be heavily burdened for a long period of time. Due to the child's special needs and huge demands, the parents may neglect their own symptoms of overload, and they can have difficulty in finding time and space to work on their own feelings.

It is quite common that the mother only becomes consciously aware of her own emotions a couple of months after the child has left the hospital. At this point help from a psychiatrist is no longer offered automatically. People can find it difficult to understand that negative emotions now suddenly appear. The child is no longer in danger, and seen from the outside, everything can appear to be idyllic, but this is not necessarily so. In any case, the reaction is often primarily connected with the earlier traumatic experiences linked to the birth and the time the child spent in hospital.

Regardless of whether it is a short or a long time after the birth, if the parents feel a need to work through their experiences, then a psychiatrist, a psychotherapist, and/or a premature parents' group can be of great help.

Parents who have their own traumatic experiences to work through, and assimilate, can find it difficult to fulfil the parental role, particularly if the child itself is traumatized.

It can be difficult to find the balance between necessary considerations for the child and too much consideration. But if, as a parent, one is aware, if one looks for information, and if one is able to sense what is right, then it is possible to achieve and maintain an equilibrium. The better balanced one is as a parent, the better one will be able to avoid instinctive and impulsive reactions;

if one has time to think through the situation, one will not react inappropriately.

Family therapy or infant therapy can offer solutions if there are difficulties with interaction in the family.

Two professional articles dealing with motherhood/parenthood in relation to premature children are Davis, Mohay, and Edwards, "Mothers' involvement in caring for their premature infants: a historical overview" (2003), and Jackson, Ternestedt, and Schollin, "From alienation to familiarity: experiences of mothers and fathers of preterm infants" (2003).

Siblings

That weekend became very long. Actually, it turned into two months. I moved about and stayed in various places and became more and more withdrawn. Very few discovered this, because I tried to hide it. I can remember that I cried a lot and wanted to be at home.

Annesofie Brock, 12-year-old sister of a hospitalized premature boy
(2000, p. 17)

Siblings of premature children are not only strongly involved in their family's difficulties in connection with the early birth, hospital stays, and eventual requirement for extended respite sessions, but they are also aware of the hidden handicaps, they notice that the baby is different from other children, and how much more it demands of the parents' resources. As this book concentrates on premature children and their latent handicaps, it will just be mentioned in passing that there may be some psychological conditions with siblings' relationships that demand extra attention and possibly therapeutic treatment. The sibling can, for instance, feel that it is in the way, ignored, guilty, or "not good enough".

A Swedish research study does, however, indicate that siblings who had earlier been in harmony and who normally live in well-functioning families will cease to show symptoms of mental and emotional difficulties once the family's burden diminishes (Stjernqvist, 1996).

Having one's children in two different places is a continual dilemma, particularly during the infant's stay in hospital. It can be very difficult to be effective in both places. Firm routine, firm agreements, the parents alternating, and assistance from the family may be part of what is needed to make things function fairly satisfactorily, both during and after the infant's stay in hospital.

Twins and triplets—siblings in the same situation

Twins or triplets who are born prematurely have a shared background in many areas, but they can develop very differently. For example, one may be handicapped, one may show delayed motor skills and/or delayed language development, one may be more fearful and insecure than its sibling(s). It is a difficult task for the parents to minister to the differing needs, to remain fair, and so on, and multiple-birth children will have a tendency to compare themselves with each other more than do other siblings. This is partly due to the tendency of people to think that as the children are of the same age, they ought to be equal in their abilities—and this rubs off on the children themselves.

The children can be supported in finding their own individual strengths and their own competences if the adults close to them avoid comparisons and, from when they are very young, get the children to accept the idea that they are independent individuals with differing needs, strengths, and weaknesses, just like everyone else, and if they emphasize that everyone is good at something, especially in a situation when one of the children is feeling frustrated because it cannot do something the other can.

Extra awareness of the child's difficulties is naturally required if one of the twins is functioning less well than the other, but it must be realized that the better functioning twin does still have a need for just as much attention.

Case histories

The following cases have been chosen from among the many approaches I have had from parents who have asked for advice. They have been selected from a desire to illustrate the variety, the frustrations, and the coping strategies adopted by the families of premature children, and to illustrate in this manner the more professional and theoretical views and opinions.

Josephine (Soenderborg)

July 2001

I am writing as a parent with a bleeding heart. You have earlier talked about Filip and Marina and their problems when they were learning to ride a bicycle. How did you tackle this?

Jaqueline, who was born in Week 32 and was 5 years old in May, must at present watch all her small friends cycling round, in many cases even without stabilizing wheels on their bicycles. For some time now, we have taken the bicycle out whenever, on rare occasions, she has wanted to practise. This rarely happens, because she is frightened as a result of her earlier failures. In this one area she is still a delicate little being, and she has *great* difficulty in distancing herself from earlier unpleasant experiences. This applies not only to cycling, but in general to many things in her daily life. We consider, however, that we have become good at finding her "balance" and that we have become good at helping/pushing her a bit along the way, so that she very often manages to cross some small frontier and thus change little failures into successes (accompanied by great delight). But we really do not want to put pressure on her using the bicycle. Little brother Marc will soon be 3 years old and is zooming around on a bike with stabilizers in the kindergarten. It pains us to watch Jaqueline in this situation, as I know the thoughts that are racing around in her head.

September 2002

Jaqueline used an incredible amount of energy and thought on the entire situation involving the bicycle; she had great difficulty in sorting things out in her head, combined with the fact that she was very frustrated over the situation.

She refused to even try the bicycle again for a long time and reacted—as most people do—by repressing and at the same time finding excuses, such as "Some children only learn to cycle when they are 10, don't they, Mum?" Jaqueline has always wanted to do things to perfection before she begins something new. This applies not only to cycling, but also to other things. In the kindergarten she used to spend much time observing the others and only dared to try something when she was certain the she could do it without difficulties.

At the same time she has an incredible need to be acknowledged and to feel good enough. (I can actually relate quite well to this—and several pieces fell into place for me about my reaction pattern in some situations—I was also born too early.)

I am convinced that this is all founded on the first few weeks, when she was separated from me. I sincerely believe that these tiny premature babies lie in their own little world and feel totally alone, abandoned, and "not good enough".

Well, as far as the cycling was concerned, the situation developed so that we left her to become ready, and one day, about 5 months ago, she decided she would like to try again. This time she became intensely irritated by the stabilizers and asked for them to be taken off. Mads removed them and took her down to a big empty car park. Suddenly I look up and see Dad come panting after Jaqueline, who is beaming, coming to meet me with a huge grin on her face. Cycling without a wobble all by herself!!! She was *very* proud of herself, and we were doubly happy.

Once again she has used a lot of time in order to be able to do it to perfection.

Now she has begun school, and this has gone much, much better than we had dared to hope. She has settled in incredibly well and is enormously good at finding playmates in school. She plays with children from the whole class and also from other classes. And she is a very popular playmate, also among the boys. According to her class teacher, they swarm round her like bees around honey.

So she has shown great development during this last year or so. We still fairly frequently experience fits of frustration and her lack of "filter". She is lacking in the ability to calm herself, which I think most other children have. So when she is upset, hurts herself, or something like that, she pours heart and soul into her feelings, with big tears streaming, and her whole world collapses during these moments. I still find this very difficult to observe and to help her. In this situation only consolation, more consolation, and big hugs seem to help, even though it can be difficult to reach her as she often switches off completely and only focuses on the thing that has just happened.

Pernille (Skanderborg)

July 2001

In 1995 I gave birth to a daughter, born 9 weeks prematurely.

My daughter is doing well today: to the outside world a bundle of energy, but as fragile as crystal internally.

I have had many bad experiences in connection with my stay in hospital, and therefore my hobbyhorse has become to attempt to improve conditions for hospitalized mothers and accompanying fathers on maternity and neonatal wards.

As one can only change a system through knowing it, I have begun to train as a nurse and plan to work with premature children when the time comes. Furthermore, I am also aiming to learn more about the hidden handicaps arising from premature birth. I—and many others parents in the same situation—feel that we are beating our heads against a brick wall when we try to draw attention to our children's "handicap".

September 2002

Our daughter is amazingly active. The only reason she isn't hyper or ADHD is actually because she is able to concentrate on things. But most of the time she races about madly.

She is frightened of anything new. Having to begin in 1st Class (Year 1), even though she had been to kindergarten (reception) and knows everyone, made her summer holiday a terror-filled experience.

She refuses to go the toilet or to buy a soft drink in any strange place, even if we are right next to her. She won't sleep away from home—and this includes both family and school friends. At home she seeks conflict beyond belief, yet at school she uses all her energy in cooperating. She is frightened of men—doctors and dentists in particular, but also other men. It took three years and a change to a female dentist to get her into the chair (despite attending habituation visits every third month). When someone leaves our house—one of us, or just a visitor—she breaks down totally and clings determinedly to people. She is very touchy, and it takes nothing at all before she feels that she is being corrected or teased. She cannot handle being different—this has something to do with self-esteem. The psychiatrist says that her self-esteem is fine, but that is not what we experience at home. We must prepare her for the changes that will happen; for example, last year we did not prepare her for the fact that it would soon be time to start wearing her all-in-one suit, so all hell broke loose, and she was sent to school wearing a thin summer jacket. The next day she wore her all-in-one suit. It is equally bad if we prepare her too long in advance.

We had been given an appointment with a cranio-sacral therapist, and we had to prepare our daughter for this. As part of this advance warning I told her about her birth, we looked at pictures, and so on. At first she became angry, really angry, over the fact that I could have left her in that glass case, and when I explained that it was a question of whether I wanted her to live or to die, she totally broke down. I do not believe I have ever experienced so deep a grief in anyone. It was a frightening experience, and it made me realize that the body remembers its traumas. It gave her a better understanding of why she reacts as she does. Often after a hysterical outburst she has cried and said "I don't know why I do it, but I can't help it." This, it must be said, is precisely right!

But she is getting older, and slowly—very slowly—we can feel that she is getting better at handling it all. She is less easily aroused, she loses her temper less often, and this makes life easier for her siblings who no longer need to be constantly on guard against another tantrum.

Susanne (Horsens)

(The names in this story are fictitious, as the persons wish to remain anonymous.)

April 2001

Dear Jonna,

Last evening I attended your lecture in Horsens. I was frightened, and the hairs on the back of my neck were bristling with anxiety as I set off—totally devoid of a desire to go. It was, after all, a type of day of judgement. What can we expect? What sort of impenetrable pedagogical work do we have to reconcile ourselves to for many, many more years. . . . I sat next to my friend. When I sat down for the lecture, I got an acute pain in my back and a sensation of tenseness in my neck. I knew it, I thought. There is no escape—now you are going to suffer a reaction again. I had experienced the reactions breaking through in the days leading up to this evening. My brother lives next door to the place where the midwife holds her clinic, and I was painting window frames for him. When I opened the window towards the place of consultation, I became upset. A few minutes later my sister-in-law switched on their baby alarm. It sounded like having the examination checking on the baby's heartbeat, I thought. So OK. . . . I knew that your lecture would cost me a constructive but "hard-work" round of working through my worries. Good thing that I had worked on self-development for more than ten years, so I know myself form top to toe. Then it is possible to bear it, after all.

But returning to last evening: when you began to speak of reactions and consequences, I felt like a 10-year-old girl had by mistake come into the cinema to see a horror film. I felt that I wanted to sit close to my friend and squeeze her hands very hard. I experienced a desire to both hear and see and, at the same time, I wanted to hide under the seat. Thank God my friend is more rational than I am, and I managed to control myself.

That evening fired my enthusiasm. First, it became much clearer to me what the problems are with our little Christina. Next, my duty as regards education became much clearer. My acceptance of the fact that, from a certain perspective, my daughter is handicapped moved a giant step forward last evening. By accepting this fact, my personal expectations of getting further support are much improved. (I have a round of hospitals and social administration facing me next week.)

Christina's birth history: Born in Week 28, with a birth weight of 706 g, and 34 cm long. She was born about 40% too small in relation to her gestational age.

Christina is our second child. She was born early because my high blood pressure reduced the amount of nourishment available to her. Our first child had been delivered at home after a totally wonderful pregnancy.

Three days later

I was at the hospital today. Here I told them of my worries about Christina's ability for sense integration. Now they will arrange a consultation with a specialist in young children.

September 2002

Christina is now 26 months old. I am on leave to care for her at home until she is 2½ years old.

Christina is, all in all, well now. She has a slight spastic paralysis in her left side, but she is mobile. Her immune system is still poor—and this will again be put to the test in the winter. She is emotionally fragile when facing new situations, loud noises, and people she does not know. On the other hand, she is a happy little girl (when she is well). She demonstrates good social understanding and interest in other children. She makes her opinions known and has sufficient self-esteem to demand her rights (when she is feeling secure!). She is good at engrossing herself in play and loves her own company. She can be lethargic and in inner peace. She is also happy at energetic games and actually has a good sense of humour and is familiar with "mental games". For instance, I'll say "boo peep" or "catch as catch can", and so on. I believe that due to her lack of development during her first 1½ years of life and her foetal development, she has learned to appreciate the quality of the small pleasures in life—actually a very positive gift for life. . . .

It has been hard work getting her to the stage of development and wellbeing she is at today. She had great problems with her development during the first 1½ years: problems with digestion, she suffered dreadful pains in her ears, she was ill a lot of the time with various infections. She was totally stressed, not only because of the early birth, but also because of the period in the womb without sufficient nourishment. She had difficulties in coping with contact and had little surplus energy for games and development. As she developed later, we found that she is visibly asymmetric in the left and right halves of the body.

We have established various methods to help her: cranio-sacral therapy, which was truly stress-relieving and helped positively with the digestive problem. Reflexology has helped to relieve some of the ear pain and eased the discomfort caused by the infections. The reflexology has also helped to strengthen her immune system, but only a little. Christina was given physiological training in connection with her asymmetrical body. It was brief, but very valuable. She was able to stand and soon began to walk. We used the "toy library" to borrow toys to train her gross motor skills. It was excellent because many of the things one can borrow are very expensive and terribly big. It would not be possible to buy them for one's own use.

We did try the "ball blanket", but she could never get used to it.

Christina was attending infant therapy at the same time as she was having cranio-sacral therapy. The cranio-sacral therapy focused on the relief of shock and stress, and the infant therapy helped by putting relevant words to the trauma. We had some therapy with themes such as the time spent in the stomach, attitude to food, attitude to pain, contact, and self-responsibility. The therapy has quite clearly had an effect, and some of the principles of the therapy have been used as a communication model that constantly puts words to causes. The good part is that the child no longer feels she has to cope with difficult things on her own.

Our life has included many people during a time when energy levels have been low or nonexistent. It has naturally been a dilemma—needing peace and quiet and at the same time needing help and assistance. Now and again it has been difficult to cope with the many demands on emotions and actions. But we have been given really good assistance, which has undoubtedly contributed to the fact that Christina is relatively well today.

Most significant of all, however, is that the child feels Mum's and Dad's presence and love—without these, the child has difficulty in mobilizing resources to enable cooperation with the helpers.

Ulla (Taastrup)

July 2000

I am the mother of a pair of 6-year-old twin boys who arrived in the world in 1994, 10½ weeks pre-term. I have been fighting an almost impossible battle against the system to get help of some kind, and the older the children have become, the more difficult it has become, because now they are so old that their "premature birth should not have any influence now". But they still do not sleep through the night. Of course there are some nights when they manage to, but time and again I wake up with at least one of them in my bed.

The fact that we have had no chance of relief has caused the relationship between their father and me to break down.

Few councils provide an auxiliary remedial teacher and the possibility of relief for parents of premature twins. I can confirm that it is a difficult period to get through! To begin with they were very ill for the first three years of their lives; we got over that, and now they have language difficulties and behavioural problems.

We have done what we could to take corrective action, but one gets worn down when there is no understanding and no help to be found anywhere other than a psychiatrist who has specialized in premature children's behaviour. And as our families did not want to help look after them because of the difficulties, we had no chance of a breathing space in the daily hubbub.

As already stated, it has cost us our relationship, and having to get a job can appear insurmountably difficult when one has not had an unbroken night's sleep (for 6 years).

September 2002

The school was the next new thing that had to be incorporated into their daily life. Caspar was not ready to join a normal class, so I had to rush to get him accepted into a special needs class where there were only 6 pupils and two teachers. Andreas, on the other hand, was 100% ready to join a normal class, which is what he did. The special class was not held at our local catchment school, so the two were separated rather abruptly, and for the two years that Casper was attending special needs class they used somewhere between half an hour and a whole hour every day to relate to one another again, typically by means of physical fights or verbal attacks on each other.

I think that these were two very difficult years when they were separated during the day, but on the other hand, it was not possible to do it any other way.

Both boys have had a need to join me at night for many years. Even now I can be awakened by one of the boys in the sitting-room watching TV in the middle of the night.

Casper and Andreas are now attending the same school, though following different syllabuses and in different classes, but they can share the breaktimes if this is what they want to do, and they are much better able to share each other's activities, and this is apparently important for my two. Both Casper and Andreas have become much nicer to each other since both have been attending the same school. And now, finally, they sleep through the night 95% of the time. At present a nightly upheaval occurs only if they are going to attend something they have been eagerly anticipating. This has given me the space to start on my teacher-training course.

We still do not get much help from the family, but the need is lessened after our divorce, as it is a relief for me when Casper and Andreas are with their father.

We have moved to a bigger place where there is room for Casper and Andreas to have their own rooms, and all in all we are generally moving towards a settled state as a family.

Iben and Joergen (Valby)

April 2001

We are the parents of Kristian, who is 2 years old, born at 28 weeks and 2 days, and Mads, who is almost 5 years old, who was born after 27 weeks and 6 days.

We have just heard from the kindergarten about the problems that Mads has, and there are many more than we thought. . . .

He has problems playing with the other children because his world is very black-and-white. If the other children do not want to play "his" game, he walks off. He has difficulties in adapting to a role, so he plays a lot on his own. (We naturally think that it is a pity!) He becomes very aggressive in various situations and allows no one to get too close (at least not other children). He seeks out adult company. He finds it difficult to understand a common request given to a group. To explain this better—one needs to have eye contact with him when the message is given. He is often very distant and difficult to reach, and he hits the other children.

The teacher considered that the "symptoms" were a consequence of his premature birth, but we didn't really consider that we got any advice to help tackle the problems at home. It was rather a lot to digest, and I had to go home and collect myself because, quite honestly, I became very upset—also because I had not been told earlier in the course. I was taken aback that I had not noticed the signals. After all, I did not think that my boy was so different. . . .

September 2002 (Luxembourg)

It has been difficult to move Mads (now 6 years old) and Kristian (now 3½ years old) to Luxembourg. Mads in particular has been very confused, aggressive, angry, and upset, because he has found it difficult to adapt to the Luxembourg system and to change kindergartens. He had to begin in kindergarten. (They begin here when they are 4 years old!) It was terribly frustrating for him, and we sought psychiatric help from Denmark. A psychiatrist who is linked to the European School was recommended to us, and we contacted him during a visit to Denmark during autumn 2001. It was simply GOLD! He has given us some tools and the courage to continue down here. He actually said that for Mads's sake we should stay here for at least five years. . . .

He recommended that we should apply for help for Mads at the school, which we did. We were allocated a social pedagogue for five hours a week to support Mads when things become a bit too much, to help by giving him advance information about what was going to happen, and in particular to be there during gymnastics and music (Mads has something about big rooms and lots of people). The extra help has meant that Mads has functioned really well. And of course the other children benefit as well by sometimes having three adults to care for the class.

We opted to be very open about our problems with Mads and among other things wrote a few pages to the parents of the children in the class, so they were given the opportunity to understand why occasionally there was an extra adult in the classroom. It resulted in a very positive response all round.

Openness about our problem has in any case been of great help, so it can really be recommended. This year Mads is beginning as a Carrot (the children are first a "pea" and then a "carrot") in the kindergarten, and we still have extra help five hours a week. We still visit the psychiatrist who also visits Luxembourg once a year. We are so lucky that he visited us privately the last time he was here.

Fortunately Mads is taking giant steps forward, such as he is beginning to draw proper drawings and play a bit more by HIMSELF. As far as motor skills are concerned, he is one of those "irritating" children who master it all with ease: for example he can ski on the red pistes and cycle 25 km without difficulty, and so on.

The reason that we have not written so much about Kristian is that he (fortunately) does not appear to have the same problems as Mads. Kristian has attended a Danish kindergarten for three half days a week for the last year or so. However, this necessitated us needing an *au pair*. And Kristian was terribly bored in the afternoons and was very upset on those days when he did not have to go to kindergarten.

Both boys attended the Commission's kindergarten full-time during the summer holidays. They have really enjoyed this, and so we have decided that Kristian shall continue there full-time. This will mean that we will not need an *au pair* and so will become more of a family. Actually we changed *au pair*s last winter as our first *au pair* returned to Denmark due to various circumstances, the most significant of which was the difficulty in handling the boys, mainly Mads. A great pity, as we were all very fond of her. However, we were very lucky in that after about a month (thorough the kind offices of Iben's mother) another *au pair* who has experience with difficult children was found. The time spent with the children is not so very different from Denmark.

The time spent at work is the same, we just begin slightly later (which gives us some much more peaceful mornings), but this unfortunately means that we return that much later.

All in all, we consider that we have settled well in Luxembourg—at last! And we would, in actual fact, have had the same problems in Denmark. It is possible that we got even more help here . . . at least on the level at which the boys are at present.

Anita (Maarslet)

September 2000

Sebastian and Andrea were born in November 1996 at 33 weeks and 2 days, by natural birth. Sebastian arrived beautifully, yelled, and was given Apgar 10. Andrea was brutally hauled out by a panicking doctor. Sebastian weighed 1,820 g, Andrea 2,035 g. They were placed into an incubator after having spent some time with us—they were not placed at the breast, nor on my stomach. I was moved to the maternity ward, my children to the neonatal ward. I was tearful and emotional as I thought it was dreadful to be separated from my children. I felt totally abandoned—and that someone had abducted my children.

The next morning I got up by myself, took a bath, and just wanted to be off. It was all so strange—one was not really happy. Well, I refused meanwhile to be separated from my children, so I insisted on moving into a room next door, which, as it happens, was empty. I did not have my children at night until they were a week old—only then was I able to sleep. The following day they were put into the incubators, as they had to have light treatment, and they were separated from me at night again for a further two nights.

Right from the start Sebastian appeared the frailer of the two: I continually felt that it was a true pity that he was born so early. He was so tiny and tender. Andrea appeared much more robust, despite the fact that she suffered from nightmares for a few months. We thought then that these were due to her brutal entry in to the world. They passed. Sebastian had to be on us, to have bodily contact—he still has. Breastfeeding was never a total success for Sebastian and me. He was not really able to get on. We were given insufficient and contradictory advice at the hospital, and actually we had all–in–all a feeling of being ignored—our children were no cause for alarm, as they were so big.

We were home two weeks after the birth, and only then did we feel happy. Lars took paternity leave for 6 months, so from that aspect we had good conditions. I only started work again once the children were 2 years old. The problems started shortly after this. Sebastian has always been a sensitive boy, a bit late in everything. He walked when he was 17 months old. He is loving, and he actively seeks physical contact.

The winter that Andrea and Sebastian had their first birthday they were continually ill, as they were again the following winter. Sebastian was always a bit more ill than Andrea, was poorly for longer, had a higher temperature, and was more affected. When he was just over 2 years old, he began to have problems with his ears. The doctors—the many duty doctors—brushed it aside. After many months of nonsense and visits to various ear specialists, the Institute for Hearing, and so on, he was finally fitted with a grommet this spring. Things are much better now. He reacts to what we say by doing what we ask him to do. He is also more contented again. But he prefers not to have conversations, and if he does reply, then only in very brief sentences. He has difficulty in handling chaotic situations, has a very low stress threshold, has a need for clarity and firm rules for every day, is withdrawn, reticent, and has difficulties in playing with other children. Not very long ago he was unable to understand/hear what the other children said. He adopted the unfortunate habit of closing down somewhat—I think he feels a bit insufficient—mostly when games demand dialogue, which the majority of games do when one is about 4 years old.

If stressed, he reacts by crying or withdrawing/going away from the sound. Noise often bothers him. He likes to romp, but it must not be too rough. His motor skills are well developed now, but he cannot/will not use the pedals on his bicycle. He has some difficulties with concentration, and he has to be firmly handled when we want him to do something (put on clothes, eat, and so on). I think that is part of the reason why it is difficult for him to join in a game.

As mentioned earlier, things are better now. Our own belief is that Sebastian's problems are caused by a combination of being born too early and having a period of impaired hearing, to what extent no one knows, and having a naturally sensitive nature.

September 2002

What has happened is that Sebastian has been "unravelled" at the children's psychiatric hospital at Risskov. He has been at the observation kindergarten and has been diagnosed as follows: infantile autism, a considerable degree of retardation, and partial epilepsy.

It has been a very difficult time, characterized by fear, endless worry, and an unending battle with the system (to get the right help).

Sebastian started in a special kindergarten on 1 November 2001. He is with a group of children who have similar difficulties. He is thriving, is contented with his daily life and experiencing a lot. Speech is still absent; perhaps it will never come. Many autistic children have no language—or at least never use it.

Sebastian had a delayed but otherwise normal development until he was 2½ years old. It was a great loss for Andrea when she eventually could not talk with him and play with him in the same way as before.

We have not focused upon the premature birth after the diagnosis was made, but we have had many thoughts about the connection between this and the autism. I wrote earlier about my experience, my perception that it was pitiful for Sebastian that he was born prematurely, that he was so frail. I still ponder a lot whether his lack of preparedness for life, his fears and fragility are contributory factors to his autism. Have they influenced the—at that time—underdeveloped centres in the brain? Could the diagnosis have been made earlier if one had been more observant and aware from the start, despite the fact that he was "only" born 7 weeks too early?

After all, being born too early is a shock for the entire system. As a mother, I still feel that it was brutality against my tiny little children to be born too early, and some can cope with it while others cannot.

I still cannot go into, or even just drive past, Skejby Hospital without getting an enormous knot in my stomach.

Kirsten and Dan (Roedovre)

October 2000

We have a son born 10 weeks too early, now 8 years old. He is in 2nd class (Year 2). No one noticed any special difficulties in the nursery school, nor in the kindergarten class. In Year 1 the school doctor noticed that he appeared unruly and a tad lacking in concentration. At the parent/school meeting, the schoolteacher hinted at more of the same/similar topics, and also mentioned that he has difficulties in acting on group instructions. The teacher is of the opinion that these problems are borderline for requiring action: maybe it is something that he will grow out of, and so on. However the doubt/uncertainty has already started to set certain alarm bells ringing in her mind.

He has difficulties in assimilating/learning. He reads fluently (better than average, compared to the rest of the class) and has no problems with arithmetic. Furthermore, he is exceptionally gifted at making music (drums). He loves playing with the other children; he is not the most popular in the class, but he is liked and is never bullied.

The problem for us is that the teacher now wants to involve the school psychiatrist—which, we of course, do not mind, as long as it will be of help to our son, but we are very determined to be included, so that we can participate in the process and not just be spectators of what the school and the school psychiatrist want to do.

September 2001

We have had a meeting with the school psychiatrist after he had observed our son for a few hours in the classroom. He could see that Kristoffer appeared socially insecure and also had difficulty in keeping his body still, appeared restless.

However, his opinion was that there was no need for further investigation as long as we, and the teachers, saw that he was progressing. So we need to see what happens.

Kristoffer is now 10 years old. Development has been very positive. He is better integrated in the group than he was previously; he is less restless, but is better able to concentrate on matters in hand. He is still happiest when he knows the rules and reacts with uncertainty, confusion, and questions, for example when the class has a "theme" week and the regular timetables are altered.

He is pleased to be given lists of things to do, as it appears that his short-term memory is not all that good. Or is he just a bit absentminded?

He is still able to keep up at school, so there is no change there. He is happy about going to school and learning new things; he is rather eager to learn.

Motor development: he is very good at both football and swimming.

The author's own diary notes

My twins were born at Week 27 + 2 days in October 1992. Briefly, both children have had a very fragile psyche, a violent fear of separation, fear of new things, experiences, and people, delayed gross motor development, stomach pains related to breakfast, problems in integrating sense-impressions, low self-esteem, and limited self-confidence.

During his first year Filip suffered from many nightmares, he did not have any bladder control, he was a "blunderer", and he had difficulties in orientating himself.

Moreover, for many years he has had frightening pictures relating to the time spent in the incubator running through his head. He has found it difficult to see things in their entirety and reacted by withdrawing into himself.

Marina has had difficulties in seeing the relationship between cause and effect, she has been mentally unbalanced, been angry, aggressive, and frustrated, and she has been very dependent on getting food at frequent intervals. As a 4-year-old she wanted to die so she could be born again!

9 July 2000

The most positive thing that has happened is a visit on 27 June 2000 with both children to a physiotherapist—Michael Cohrt—who has a private practice. By means of cranio-sacral therapy he has enabled the cerebral-spinal fluid to flow freely, which has meant that right and left hemispheres of the brain now are able to work together. The result is that Marina is happy as never before: no more frustrations, anger, and aggression resulting from sense overstimulation. She laughs at things that she would have cried over before, is drinking more water, she eats more in the morning without getting tummy ache and no longer needs so many "between-meal" snacks.

Filip is significantly better at controlling his bladder, is frequently dry all night, has gained a markedly better control of his gross motor skills, and his ability to orientate himself is markedly improved.

Both children are now able (as a rule) to write letters that face in the right direction, they have begun to play cards and lay out solitaire, and they have in general made gains in courage and self-confidence that they did not have before.

For the first time (apart from Fillip and Marina's big sister), I am experiencing having "normal" children—it's a dance on roses!

The children's normal needs (including the social and emotional ones) are now easier to deal with. Our life together is positive all day long, and it gives a huge energy surplus.

13 September 2000

Filip and Marina are well and, generally speaking, happy at school. Marina frequently experiences little difficulties when she feels that she is unable to cope with demands. She is a perfectionist and gets deeply distressed if she does not understand something or is unable to do something. But she is generally happy, and she does not have many days of being overstimulated and stressed. She still has a great need of knowing in advance what is going to happen, but we have learned to handle this, and the teachers have also become good at it. This means that, for instance, these days she'll pack to get ready to go to school camp without any worries other than whether she is allowed to bring more than one stuffed toy animal along. This is definitely progress!

Filip does not have any reservations—he packs with great enthusiasm. He has gained almost total control over his bladder now, including during the night. He is always happy and content and a real little (big!) clever Dick. He reads everything, including English and a little Latin. Right at the moment he is reading the *Guinness Book of Records*, and he has reached the section on Industry. He loves to cuddle and pet and is overall very caring. So is Marina, but her ability to encompass others and their feelings does depend on her own state of equilibrium. Filip is actually always well balanced.

Today they have left for school camp, and there were no problems with anticipatory insecurity in connection with the new and unpredictable. Both we and the school have made a great effort to prepare the children for what will happen at the school camp, but it is still a sign of progress that they did not worry in advance of leaving.

Visit to Michael Cohrt, 3 January 2001

Michael Cohrt found some "stiff" ligaments in Marina's liver/abdominal areas, and he found a form of connective tissue between the lungs. He said that this was a result of her lung illnesses, but he did not think that they were the result of RSD nor of respirator treatment but, rather, a result of RS virus and whooping cough!

He treated this partly by pulling the ligaments by means of external pressure, partly by putting firm pressure on the lung area while Marina drew in a deep breath and then releasing the pressure very quickly.

Filip's cranium was still a little unaligned, but not much in comparison with the way it had been before. He also had an imbalance in the liver area, which was treated with pressure, but it was in a different place to Marina's and was a different type of pressure. The area had connection to the urine system, and when Filip had to go to bed that night, he insisted on sleeping without a nappy! Michael checks the coordination between the brain hemispheres at each visit, and it is 100% in both children.

Visit to Michael Cohrt, 7 March 2001

Marina has had a long period of marked tiredness, lack of appetite, and depression. Michael found a skewed bone in the lowest part of the spine, where Marina had already complained of having pain. He pushed the bone into place with a little shove and also treated Marina's liver area and head. Marina got a headache from the treatment, and we had to have another visit to Michael a couple of days later. But her tiredness, lack of appetite, and lack of zest for life disappeared like dew under the sun. Filip was generally fine, but he had a few difficulties in carrying out his cross-over exercises. We asked to do these exercises at home for the next three months.

Visit to Michael Cohrt, 10 April 2001

Filip was checked all over and was "discharged". He has, by the way, slept without a nappy at night and without any accidents for almost two months, and he is functioning well in all areas.

Marina has had a lot of pain in the head and was given a thorough treatment for some blockages in the neck and the bridge of her nose. After this treatment the headaches disappeared.

13 April 2001

The children's father and I have agreed that it would be a good idea to talk with Marina about the beginnings of her life as a therapeutic method to overcome her mental problems.

I told her about how the birth went, her transfer to Rigshospitalet, and the move back to Holbæk. I made much of the details: in particular, I stressed that the separation was very much against everyone's wishes, but that it was necessary for her survival. I told her that I was not able to drive, but I missed her dreadfully. I also told her that her father was with her, and that we fought a courageous battle with the doctors to get her quickly back to Holbæk. And, finally, how very joyful I was when she finally came back.

When I had finished, she said, "So that is probably why I always miss you so much, Mummy!" And then she tucked herself in near me all evening until she had to go to bed.

Until that day Marina had rejected me with an aggressive sound and movement when I wanted to tuck her duvet in around her while she slept. But after our talk she reacted to the same situation by smiling in her sleep.

It was not only during sleep that Marina showed anger and aggression towards me. She would sometimes also reject me when I wanted to comfort or quieten her, and there was a very personal anger in her eyes on those occasions.

For me it is a clear indication that the anger Marina subconsciously felt against me was caused by the early betrayal due to the separation, and it disappeared from one moment to the next.

Her acceptance that I had been away from her because it was unavoidable, and not because I wanted to, was invaluable.

25 July 2001

During the years Marina and Filip have had a lack of self-confidence and a fear of repeating fiascos. There were many things that they did not try, or attempt again, because it had not gone too well at earlier attempts. It took an eternity to get them first to ride on bicycles with stabilizing wheels, and later to get them to cycle without the stabilizers.

We gently pushed them onwards, and they did experience small successes. But it was only once they had begun treatment and their sense impressions were integrated that something really happened. Almost from one day to the next they found it easier to face the day and the experiences it brought. They find everything in their daily life easier—they are better at understanding long explanations and seeing the connection between cause and effect. They were also more spatially aware, found it easier to carry out complex movements (do somersaults, roller-skate, and so on), gained better control over their bodies/motor skills, were better able to handle loud noises and disturbances at large gatherings. As all these daily occurrences now demanded a lot less energy and they at the same time experienced that they could do a lot of things, we moved into a positive spiral where they dared to try more and more things. And we are still in this happy state of affairs.

Almost daily we were surprised by their courage and new achievements. For example, not so long ago Marina would have approached a bouncy castle in a public place most hesitantly, she would have crept onto one corner of the cushion and begun to gently hop until she became accustomed to it. If too many children joined in, she would leave again. On St. John's Eve we were at a place with two bouncy castles of differing heights. There was a little set of stairs, which the children could use to climb onto the cushion. Marina made her entry by taking a run at it and trying to jump onto the highest cushion in one corner. She almost succeeded, and then she gently slid down the side. The she ran back, took another run, and succeeded at the second try. Such an experience can make one's heart overflow with joy.

Previously, if we looked at Marina when she was attempting to do something or other, she would generally react by becoming mildly aggressive and surly and would at once stop what she was doing. She did not want to be observed, because "just think if she did not do it properly or not well enough". Today when I look at her, she looks back with big eyes and smiles roguishly.

Fillip's self-confidence is just great. The most recent thing he has done which surprised us was to throw himself completely without inhibition into the swimming pool and to dive wearing goggles. He has always been frightened of getting water on his face, and until very recently (8½ years old) we had to help him to wash his hair.

19 February 2002

Filip,[1] who now is 9 years old, was born at Week 27 + 2 days. His neonatal and general progress are not significant in this description, but it is relevant to mention that he was in an incubator for about a month and needed quite a lot of treatments to start with. Many blood samples were taken from his heel and many drips inserted. And now I am going to skip to the next relevant experience. Until he reached the age of 1, Filip often suffered from nightmares. He would wake bathed in sweat, screaming with panic, and fear showing in his face, and he would be difficult to reach.

The dreadful nightmares began to lessen, but Filip has always been frightened of the dark and frightened of screens that close him in, and he has had unpleasant fantasies when he had to go to sleep in the evenings.

And then a big leap forward to the summer of 2001, when we were on holiday. Filip got out of bed and explained that he could not sleep because he could not get the dreadful pictures to go away. He would not tell us what the pictures were. I spent a very long time trying to get him to open up and at last succeeded. He was experiencing something that he had experienced many times before, each time almost identical images: he was lying in a glass coffin, was surrounded by strong white light. Near the coffin was the man with the scythe and some evil dark figures who could fly. All the dark shapes had sharp and pointed weapons. In the background was the black castle that they guarded.

But there were also some angels around the coffin, and the archangel Michael fought with his sword of light against the man with the scythe and the dark shapes. As long as Filip lay in the glass coffin with the strong, white light around him, he was safe, but he was still frightened.

The scene has been enacted in Filip's head many times, and he has been so frightened that he did not dare talk about it. It was liberation for him when he finally managed to talk about it.

The next morning Filip drew it all on a piece of paper, which we burned and buried in the ground. Following this there was a long period without the images, but they resurfaced at regular intervals—the last time a week ago when we had just moved into a new house.

One evening, as Filip and I were talking about the experiences he had in the incubator in quite a different context, he suddenly said, "Of course. That is what I see in my dream pictures. The glass coffin is the incubator, all the dark shapes are those that are always pricking and cutting me, the man with the scythe is death that is in ambush, and Michael is my guardian angel! I should have thought about that a bit sooner."

I will let the image remain . . .

The acceptance has been very positive for Filip, but the traumas are still so deep that we all work on them with professional help in the shape of sandplay therapy.

December 2003

The course of sandplay therapy has completely removed Filip's frightening dream images and given him inner security and strength as well as more self-esteem and self-confidence. He does experience inner peace now, but he can still be reticent in certain areas.

In recent sessions of sandplay therapy Marina has shown that many of her traumas have been assimilated and accepted along the road—for example, by her extrovert personality as well as by our conversations about the early separation. Her self-esteem and self-confidence have been much improved, and she has a well-adjusted courage to try new things.

NOTE

1. Published in *Livsbladet 1* (2002): 10–11.

CHAPTER EIGHT

Research

> Every approach to research is value-skewed. There is no neutral research.
>
> S. Brostrøm (2002, p. 10)

A great deal of research has been carried out into the various areas of premature children's development. Apart from covering a few Danish investigations, I am summarizing the main points from some of the most recent Norwegian and Swedish research projects, as conditions in these countries are comparable to those in Denmark. In addition, I refer briefly to a single international investigation and give references for some other such investigations.

As far as intelligence evaluation is concerned the tests used are based on the traditional perception of the concept of intelligence, and the researcher's conclusions must be considered with this in view. When evaluating the results of an intelligence test, it is important to be aware of the age of the testing method. In today's information society children have a tendency to develop earlier, which is why a test method can give too high a result (Stjernqvist, 1999).

Test results of quantitative investigations show the children's present condition, but they do not consider what support and follow-up the individual child has received before, or during, its participation in the investigation. This could be, for example, social, emotional, therapeutic, and/or learning support—that is, a broad spectrum, which may have a great influence on the child's development.

Therefore, when the test results show children who become worse or better as the years pass, we do not know precisely what lies behind these data.

When one analyses the follow-up studies, one must bear in mind that continuing development within neonatology and birth techniques has taken place during the years that have passed since the children's birth.

Ultrasound examinations at Week 17–18 give a greater certainty for the exact determination of the date the child will be full-term. Prevention and treatment of RDS (respiratory distress syndrome) has significantly improved during the 1990s. Increased knowledge of, for example, the need to balance oxygen supply, the need for extra proteins, pain awareness and easing of pain, as well as reduction of other stress factors may have contributed to the drop in occurrences of cranial haemorrhages.

However, with the knowledge we are gaining from the research, a new series of questions arise:

— Are the results for children born 10–20 years ago relevant to children who are born prematurely today?
— How will the children fare later? Will they, when demands are increased, fall ever further behind in comparison with other children?
— How will their behavioural difficulties influence their social competence during their youth and as adults?
— Would improved treatment and care in the neonatal period reduce the risk of ADHD and learning difficulties?
— Can one identify divergent development earlier so that one can intervene earlier?

In other words, it takes many years between introducing new treatment and knowing the consequences. But for those children and young people who were born prematurely in the 1980s and 1990s, late-developing handicaps are, for most, a fact of life today. Those children and youngsters who suffer from consequences of their premature birth have a need for extra effort and support—today.

And those premature children born within the last five years do actually still seem to have the same problems when one reads many interviews with and descriptions written by parents of premature children. It is important to keep in mind the preventative factor in neonatal care and treatment, but close monitoring and early intervention are just as important focal turning points.

Born too early—What has happened since?
(Stjernqvist, 1999)

Karin Stjernqvist's book, published in 1999, covers a psychological examination of 129 children born at Universitetssjukhuset in Lund. The children were born before 29 full weeks of gestation during 1985–86. Of these children, 65 survived; 61 of them participated in the investigation at 10 years old.

Objective

To evaluate a group of prematurely born children as part of a wider perspective, including health, intelligence, behaviour, school situation, school results, and self-perception.

Method

Examination of all children belonging to Universitetssjukhuset Lunds Southern Region born prior to Gestation Week 29 during 1985–86.

Group A consisted of 129 children, of whom 65 survived the newborn stage; 61 children (36 girls, 25 boys) and their parents participated in a comprehensive follow-up when the children were 10 years old.

Group B was a control group of a corresponding number of children born at term.

The average point of birth of Group A was after 27 full gestation weeks, and the average birth weight was 1,040 g.

At the age of 10 the children completed a questionnaire entitled "I consider that I am". On a scale from 1–4, they answered questions about their physical abilities, talents/skills, mental wellbeing, relationship to the family, as well as relations with friends and teachers.

The children's teachers filled in a questionnaire about school presentation. On a scale of 1–5, they evaluated the children's knowledge of Swedish, English, mathematics, and orientation. The teachers did not know the children's birth week.

At the age of 10 a special perception test was carried out.

Results of the investigation

Of the children in Group A, 8% had major neurological damage, including severe vision impairment or blindness, severe hearing loss or deafness, much reduced functionality or spastic paralysis, and/or mental retardation.

Almost 50% of Group A had a need for spectacles, most often because of myopia, but only some 8% of Group B had this need.

The children in Group A had several infections during their first years of life. At the age of 4 they visited the doctor more often and were more often admitted to hospital, but by the age of 10 the neurologically fit children in Group A were not ill more often nor visited their doctor more often than did Group B children,

At the age of 4 the children from Group A were on average 7 cm shorter than the children in Group B, and on average they weighed 4 kg less. Only three children from Group A had a strongly deviant height or weight development.

By the age of 10 the children in Group A weighed 4 kg less (33 versus 37 kg) and were 5 cm shorter (142 versus 147 cm).

During their first year the very premature children had eating and sleep problems. By the age of 1, the first signs of hyperactivity could be detected, and in the middle of the preschool age 40% of the very premature children showed signs of high levels of activity, whereas the eating and sleep problems were over by this time.

Of Group A, 85% had a level of development within the normal parameters, but many were in the lower range of this area. The group as a whole had a lower average than that of Group B.

The children in Group A showed a somewhat lower cognitive development than could have been expected from inheritance and environment.

In Group A, 25% were intelligent (IQ over 100), against 70% in Group B.

The children in Group A showed immaturity of perception. At the age of 10 they were, on average, at a level that would correspond to the age of 8.

In Group A, 20% had ADHD (Attention Deficit Hyperactivity Disorder), against 8% in Group B.

In Group A, 33% had behavioural difficulties, were extroverted or frightened/reticent, against 10% in Group B.

In Group A, the children showed a little increase in social problems, including a preference for playing with younger friends.

Of Group A, 92% attended a normal school; 8% were in a class for special educational needs or in a special school.

In Group A, 30% were being given special teaching, as against only 2% in Group B.

In Group A, 33% were below or very much below their expected levels in school (Swedish, English, mathematics, orientation), against 10% of Group B. Group A showed most difficulties in mathematics and English.

There were no differences between the two groups regarding self-perception—possibly due to good support from the adults to the prematurely born, and due to the children's ability to adapt to their own expectations.

Conclusion

Karin Stjernqvist considers the results of the investigation as being very positive, based upon the consideration that the participating children were unlikely to have survived if they had been born 10 years earlier, and that they had a harsh start in life, with much illness.

She points out the importance of the care that these children and their families need for early support as early as the first year of life. She is, further, of the opinion that the children's development should be closely monitored during the preschool age with a view, in cooperation with the parents, to supplying all needed support and resources to those who require them.

Psychological status at the age of 8–9
of children of birth weight under 1,501 g
(Ulvund, Smith, & Lindemann, 2001)

Objective

The aim of this investigation by Stein Erik Ulvund, Lars Smith, and Rolf Lindemann was to find out whether there were differences in the occurrence of intellectual delay, behavioural difficulties, and learning problems in children with a birth weight of less than 1,501 g and children of a higher birth weight.

Method

The very-low-weight children were born at Weeks 24–28, with Week 27 as average; the others were born at Weeks 29–34, with Week 30 as average.

The experimental group consisted of 104 children (53 girls/51 boys) who were monitored to the age of 8, with a follow-up investigation at age 9.

There was no control group in the investigation. Some of the results have, however, been compared with the relevant norm values.

The researchers elected to focus upon the differences between the more- and the less low-weight children; they therefore divided the investigated group into two:

Group A: Gestational age <28 weeks, number of children: 36;

Group B: Gestational age >28 weeks, number of children: 68.

The children were tested using the Stanford–Binet intelligence scale and with the Kaufman Assessment Battery for Children, which is a somewhat dated intelligence test, revised in 1983 and in 1986. In addition, reading, writing, and mathematical abilities were tested. Hyperactivity was tested by means of video recordings and questionnaires completed by the parents.

Results of the investigation

The most frequently occurring problems were AD/H—that is, hyperactivity and difficulties with concentration—which was found in 27% of all the children. Of Group A, 22% were hyperactive, against 32% of Group B; this indicates a surprisingly significantly *lower* occurrence of hyperactivity being shown by children born extremely early.

At the first investigation, 59% of the children from the entire group (104 children) were hyperactive. The following investigation was done at the age of 5, and 28% of the children were hyperactive at both investigations—that is, there was a significant decrease during the preschool age.

The collective results showed a moderate degree of intellectual delay and learning difficulties, but a significant difference between the two groups in favour of Group B.

It was interesting that out of 6 children born at Week 25, only a single child showed an IQ score below normal,

There were no appreciable group differences of the children's memories.

With the exception of mathematical skills, where the boys showed better comprehension than did the girls, no significant gender differences were found.

The researchers' interpretations

Those children who survive the neonatal period without major damage and who are testable show, by and large, a satisfactory intellectual development and school skills, but an earlier gestational age (not necessarily growth retardation) increases the risk of later difficulties.

Even though the authors conclude that intelligence development and school subject presentation are satisfactory, it is worrying that 27% of the children showed behavioural difficulties pertaining to concentration and hyperactivity (ADHD), and even more did so in the earlier preschool age. It is also worrying that the extremely premature children have a markedly higher degree of intellectual delay and learning difficulties.

But the question is, can we accept these results, as the researchers have opted to use Dubowitz's method of determining gestational age. This method is based on an examination of the child after birth, which has been shown to be unreliable in the case of extremely prematurely born children.

The ETFOL Five-Year Investigation, 2002

In 2002 physician Bo Mølholm Hansen and psychiatrist Barbara Hoff, Rigshospitalet, carried out a countrywide ETFOL investigation[1] (Post investigation of children born extremely early and with low weight) at the request of the Danish Paediatric Neonatal Committee (Dansk Pædiatrisk Selskabs neonataludvalg).

The investigation included 252 5-year-old children born in 1994 and 1995 with a birth weight of ≤ 1,000 g, or born before the end of Gestational Week 28.

A control group of 76 full-term children was included.

The children were investigated at 5, 12, and 24 months and again at 5 years of age.

Background

At the end of the 1980s there was an intense debate in Denmark among both public and physicians regarding the treatment of children born extremely early. The discussion covered whether the risk of hidden handicaps was too high to justify treatment of the children, and follow-up studies of premature children were requested to throw light on this area. The treatment of breathing difficulties among extremely prematurely born children in Denmark is significantly different from methods used elsewhere. Early Nasal CPAP is common, and respirator treatment is therefore used much less than in other countries.

The ETFOL study was initiated to evaluate (among other things) how extremely prematurely born children treated according to Danish principles progressed in the long term.

Method

Out of 269 surviving children from the ETFOL study, 252 were investigated at 5 years of age.

The investigation gave priority to an overview of the entire group of children from ETFOL. The design of the investigation consisted primarily of a questionnaire, a psychological development test, and a motor-skill development test.

The psychological development test used was WPPSI–R (Wechler's Preschool and Primary Scale of Intelligence—Revised). The children were allocated a combined IQ score on the basis of a background of a series of tasks.

The motor-skill development test was based on the Movement Assessment Battery for Children. The purpose of the test was to provide a more detailed assessment of the children's motor-skill development.

Based on the test results, the children were placed into three groups:

1. children without motor-skill difficulties;
2. children with motor-skill difficulties;
3. children on the borderline between the two groups above.

The results of the test were compared with those of a group of 76 children born at term (control group).

The children's social and behavioural development was investigated by means of questionnaires.

Results of the investigation

• *Care.* Almost all of the 252 ETFOL children attended a nursery school and were therefore looked after outside their homes:

— 81% attended a normal nursery school without special educational provision;
— 12% attended a normal nursery school and had help from a support teacher for a varying number of hours weekly;
— 7% were looked after in a special institution or had a special place in a normal nursery school.

It is not possible to find a reliable basis for comparison, as collective statistics of children in Denmark who receive support at the preschool age are not available. An educated *guess* is 5%.

• *Motor-skill development*: Almost 10% of the ETFOL children had cerebral pareses, mainly of the spastic kind. There was a great difference in the range of motor-skill disturbances as well as any accompanying developmental disturbances; 2.5% of the children had no independent walking function.

The children without cerebral pareses and without severe visual deficiency—21 ETFOL children and 76 controls—participated in the motor-skill development test (see also vision and hearing, below).

Of those ETFOL children who participated in the test, 58% were classified as being without motor problems, 19% had motor difficulties, and 23% were in the borderline area.

The control group passed the tests as expected: 83% of the control children were classified as being without motor difficulties, 1% had motor difficulties, and 16 % were in the border area.

• *Vision and hearing:* Among the ETFOL children, 5% had reduced vision (corrected visual acuity less than 0.3); 1% of the children were blind (corrected acuity less than 0.1).

There were no severely hearing-deficient children.

• *Intellectual development:* Based upon the results of the control group, the ETFOL children's IQ scores were as follows:

— 19% below normal area;

— 22% low in normal area;

— 51% in the middle of the normal area;

— 7% high in the normal area;

— 1% above the normal area.

• *Social and behavioural development.* Several of the ETFOL children had immature social skills and/or exhibited inattentive and hyperactive behaviour. There was, however, a connection between, on the one hand, intellectual development below average and, on the other, immature social skills as well as inattentive and hyperactive behaviour.

ETFOL children with a normal intellectual development were no different from the control children with regard to their social skills and their behavioural development.

Summary

Evaluated at 5 years of age:

— Most of the ETFOL children showed normal development.

— Individually, the children were different, just like other children.

— Considered as a group, extremely premature children are more vulnerable than children born at term; more of these children show developmental disturbances.

The results from the ETFOL Five-Year Investigation cannot be applied to all prematurely born children, as the risk of hidden handicap is greater in the most immature and smallest children.

Parts of the ETFOL five-year investigation have been published in overseas journals[2]:

— "The Danish National Study in Infants with Extremely Low Gestational Age and Birth Weight (the ETFOL study): Respiratory Morbidity and Outcome" (Kamper, Feilberg Jorgensen, Jonsbo, Pedersen-Bjergaard, & Pryds, 2004).

— "Early Nasal Continuous Positive Airway Pressure in a Cohort of the Smallest Infants in Denmark: Neurodevelopmental Outcome at Five Years of Age (Hansen, Greisen, & Mortensen, 2004).

— "Perinatal Risk Factors of Adverse Outcome in Very Preterm Children: A Role of Initial Treatment of Respiratory Insufficiency?" (Hansen, Hoff, et al., 2004).

Intelligence in Preterm Children at Four Years of Age as a Predictor of School Function
(Hansen, Dinesen, Hoff, & Greisen 2002)

Aims of the investigation

The study was performed in order to investigate whether premature children of very low birth weight (VLBW) showed reduced school performance beyond that explained by the deficit in intelligence score at 4 years of age.

Background

Handicaps such as spastic paralysis (*cerebral pareses*), blindness, impaired hearing, and severe learning difficulties can generally occur within the first five years of life. But many of the skills that are of significance for future functions cannot be judged at this age.

Intelligence measurements can be carried out from the age of 4–6.

A lower IQ score is found in children with VLBW compared to children of normal birth weight (NBW), though the majority do lie within the norm. The difference seems to persist to the age of 10–12 years and implies a lack of support in the period after preschool age.

School results can be taken as a yardstick for learning difficulties, which are often first apparent at the ages of 8–10.

The investigators expected to find that the markedly lower IQ score for children with VLBW would result in an increased risk of problems at school. The main objective of the investigation was to determine whether school performance was reduced in children of low birth weight above what could be ascribed to the lower IQ score at the age of 4.

Method

Examinations were conducted of 333 4-year-old children, followed by telephone interviews with the same children (257) when they had grown up (at the ages of 18–20). The investigation evaluated the school performance in a cohort of children with VLBW following the primary-school period. It was a long-term study with control-group participation.

Cohorts

A. Very low birth weight (VLBW): <1,501 g
    (102 children at age 4; 79 young people at age 18–20)
B. Low birth weight (LBW): >1,500 g and <2,300 g
    (139 children at age 4; 114 young people at age 18–20)
C. Normal birth weight (NBW): 2,500 g
    (92 children at age 4; 64 young people at age 18–20)

Gender at age 18–20: 47% girls, 53% boys.

Test model at age 4:
    CGI (Cognitive General Index) from McCarthy's Scales of Children's Abilities.

Test model at age 18–20:
> 1. school difficulties, defined as a combination of special education and at most 9 years school attendance, and
> 2. results of Year 11 final examination.

The children with VLBW were examined at the age of 2 and again at the age of 4, where the children with LBW as well the control group with NBW were included in the cohort.

The 333 participants who took part in the investigation as 4-year-olds were contacted by letter once they were aged 18–20, following which a telephone interview was carried out with 288 participants; 257 of those interviewed were included in the analysis.

The first part of the telephone interview concerned life quality. The second part concerned school experiences and included the following questions:

1. Was there a need for special education or a special school?
2. The average level of marks after the Year 11.
3. Education after leaving the primary school.

The interviewer knew neither details of birth date nor the results from the investigation at age 4.

Results of the investigation

At age 4 the intelligence score was 103.7 for children with VLBW, 110.5 for children with LBW, and 117.3 for children with NBW.

Problems with schooling were reported for 42% of the children with VLBW, 25% of children with LBW, and 17% of children with NBW.

The more frequently occurring problems with schooling in children with VLBW occurred also in those children who had neurological problems.

The children with VLBW, who in addition (via their parents) also belonged to a socioeconomic risk group, had a significantly higher risk of school problems than did the other groups. An extremely low IQ score at age 4 was a great risk factor for future school performance.

The data that were available from birth—socioeconomic status, gender, and birth-weight group—were all significant and independent in the prediction of school performance, but this only explained 13% of the differences between the youngsters' skills. When the result from the IQ tests were added, the explanatory part of the differences was increased to 28%, but birth-weight group and genetics no longer had an independent relevance on the prediction of preparedness for school.

A median or high score at the age of 4 appears, according to the researchers, to protect against school problems. A high socioeconomic status is also a predictor of good school skills.

The results indicated that two children with the same IQ and same social background at the age of 4 had the same risk of school difficulties, regardless of whether the birth weight was below 1,500 g or was normal.

The investigators' conclusion

The research team consider that their results indicate that specific difficulties with regard to learning and difficulties with attention/concentration are linked to a low IQ score in children with LBW. Even though the problems only become apparent at school, they have, according to the researchers, no influence on school abilities. This could be because they could be the result of the same neurological disturbances that are the cause of the children's low IQ score. This supposition is supported by several others, who point out that children with VLBW suffer more often from sensory-integration problems.

The researchers suggest that possible side effects of new methods of nursing and treatment methods and their influence on brain development should be investigated as early as possible.

The researchers point out that it is a weakness in the investigation that specific learning difficulties and attention disturbances in children of school age were not evaluated directly. They point out, furthermore, that the clinical reliability of a one-day evaluation of children at the age of 4–5 years is doubtful. Finally, the research team mention that IQ scores do not describe strengths and weaknesses, and that these should be analysed to find compensating factors of significance for the learning process. This is a dynamic process based on trust between the child, the family, and the professionals.

Follow-Up investigation of 9–10-year-old children born in North Jutland County 1988/89
(Agerholm, 1999)

Departmental physiotherapist Hanne Agerholm and special occupational therapist Berit Roed, both at the children's department, Aalborg Hospital North, carried out an examination of 57 children at the age of 3–4 years and of the same children (50) at the age of 9–10 years.[3]

The children had a birth weight of ≤1,500 g; the average birth weight was 1,270 g (697–1,500 g). The mean birth week was 30.6 weeks (26th–37th week), and the gender distribution was 30 girls and 20 boys.

Defined objectives of the investigation

To find the answers to the following questions:

1. What is the frequency of handicap of 9–10-year-olds with a birth weight of ≤1,500 g of children born in North Jutland County compared with the investigation carried out when the children were 3–4 years old?

2. Are the differences in the distribution of the defined two groups in the two investigations?

3. How have those children fared who were being monitored for developmental problems?

4. What can be predicted from examinations carried out on a 3–4-year-old?

5. Are the procedures used with regard to prematurely born children sufficiently effective, or should we change the practice?

The children were divided into the following groups

A. *Normal children* with age-corresponding motor skills and perceptual and social development—for example, no sensorimotor, cognitive, or behavioural difficulties.

B. *Children under observation* for behavioural problems defined by deficiency in relation to normal development, but without need for remedial help.

C. *Children with lesser handicap* defined by comparison to normal development with requirement for remedial help, or with an isolated handicap, where the children are helped by their own efforts.

D. *Children with serious handicaps* defined by retarded psychomotor development as compared to normal development, and with a need for special help arrangements of a wide-ranging type.

Results of the investigation

At the 9–10-year investigation, the categorization was as follows:

A. 23 children (46%) were normal, compared with 38 (67%) at the age of 3–4 years;

B. 11 children (22%) with motor-skill difficulties or delayed motor-skill development were under observation for developmental problems, compared with 8 children (14%) at 3–4 years of age; the children coped well with everyday life and had no extra support at school;

C. 10 children (20%) had a minor handicap in the shape of motor problems and learning difficulties, as compared with 7 children (12%) at 3–4 years of age;

D. 6 children (12%) had a serious handicap, against 4 children (7%) at 3–4 years of age.

These comparisons were done against the background of the total number of children included in the two investigations. There were 7 fewer children in the 9–10 years of age investigation (see Figure 8.1).

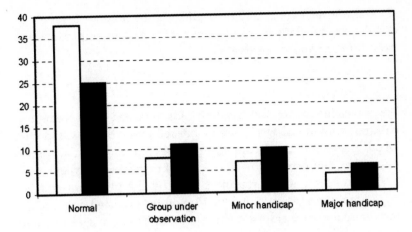

FIGURE 8.1.   Grouping of total number of children involved in the two studies. Key: ☐ 3–4 years old; ■ 9–10 years old

Conclusion

Follow-up investigation of children aged 9–10, born in Nordjylland County, 1988/89, bw ≤1,500 g: significantly more of the children showed delayed development at the ages of 9–10 when compared to the results of the investigation carried out at the ages of 3–4 years.

Of the children, 13 who had been judged as normal at the age of 3–4 years were moved to the observation and minor handicap groups. Only one child was moved from the group under observation to the normal group, and one child remained in the observation group. The others were moved from the observation group to the minor and serious handicap groups.

The children in the minor and serious handicap groups remained in their groups.

The clear connection between delayed/deficient development at the age of 3–4 years and at the age of 9–10 years indicates that the children do not outgrow their developmental problems, and there are, in addition, increasing developmental problems in step with increasing age. These conditions underline the need for follow-up to school age with the object of clarification of developmental problems as well as an early supportive effort with regard to known developmental deficiencies.

The normal group is altered with the increasing demands of developmental skills related to age, which further emphasizes the need for continuous observation.

Procedure

The investigation of the 3–4-year-olds revealed that premature children born at <32 weeks are monitored today by the Children's Department, Aalborg Hospital, until they are 5 years old; previously they had been followed only until they were 1½ years old.

The children attend routine checks by the physician and occupational therapist at 5, 9, and 13 months' adjusted age, and by the occupational therapist or physiotherapist at the ages of 3 and 5 years.

At the 3-year examination the MPU test (Motor Perceptual Development) is used. This correctly identified 14 out of 15 children with developmental problems at the 3–4-year stage. It provides a broad overview of the child's ability level.

At the 5-year examination a cognitive test, combined with the MAP-test (Miller Assessment for Preschoolers), is recommended, because the type of scoring system used can be compared to other investigations of children at preschool and school age.

Behavioural problems in children who weigh 1,000 g or less at birth in four countries
(Hille et al., 2001)

The first combined European–American investigation was published in 2001, under the direction of the Dutch physician Elysée T. M. Hille.

The investigation involved 408 8–10-year-old children, born in Holland, Germany, the United States, and Canada, and with a birth weight of ≤1,000 g.

Method

The investigation was built on the parents' replies to questionnaires, and it showed common traits in the premature children across countries and continents. The investigation included a matched control group of children born at term. The total control group includes four cohorts.

The investigation was built up as a main problem score with eight sub-scales.

1. two of these—aggressive and defiant behaviour—give a collected score on outwardly reacting behaviour;

2. three of these—fearful, somatic, and reticent behaviour—give a collected score on inwardly reacting behaviour;

3. three others—disturbed attention, as well as social and mental problems—indicate problems that do not fit into the other groups.

Results of the investigation

Children with an extremely low birth weight have, on the whole, a higher score than the control group, but the difference was only significant in the European countries. (Almost all restless and hyperactive schoolchildren in the United States have their symptoms reduced by medication that stimulates the central nervous system.)

Scores in the individual eight scales were only higher for the extremely small children in the Group 3 and Group 2 cohorts. In summary, one can say that there was an over-representation of children with an extremely low birth weight who had:

— more difficulties with concentration;

— greater problems in thinking clearly and logically;

— more problems interacting with others.

A single group of the very small children (Holland) were more fear-filled and reticent and showed somatic symptoms.

There were significantly more boys with behavioural difficulties, most markedly from the European countries.

Despite cultural differences, the types of behavioural problems of extremely low birth-weight children were very similar in all four countries, which the investigators interpreted as that the biological mechanisms appear to be contributory to behavioural difficulties in children with an extremely low birth weight.

The researchers' conclusion

In order to avoid learning difficulties and to help the children better to master social interaction with other children, it is important to monitor and support those prematurely born children who have a need of this.

Quality of life in young adults with very low birth weight (Dinesen & Greisen, 2001)

S. J. Dinesen and G. Greisen, Neonatalafdelingen, Rigshospitalet, carried out a telephone interview investigation of 280 young people aged 18–20 years who were born in 1980–82.

Defined goals of the investigation

The aim was to measure the quality of life of a group of young adults born with a very low birth weight (<1,500 g) in 1980–82 and to compare these with a control group with a normal birth weight and a corresponding cohort born eight years earlier. The investigation was important, because survival during those years increased rapidly to 81% in 1980–82, compared with 48% eight years earlier. The higher survival rates were due to more intensive treatment, and one could worry that the result would be that more children survived with handicaps and a more difficult life.

Cohorts

1. very low birth weight (VLBW): <1,500 g (92 persons);
2. low birth weight (LBW): >1,500 g and <2,500 g (119 persons);
3. normal birth weight (NBW): >2,500 g (69 persons).

• *Test model*: Telephone interview by means of structured questionnaire developed from Aggernæs' theories (see below).

The investigation was compared with a similar investigation of a group of young adults born in 1971–74 with a very low birth weight.

The group with VLBW was examined at the age of 2, and all three groups were examined at the age of 4. Children with VLBW and LBW who had a handicap or chronic illness were placed into separate groups and analysed separately and are therefore not included in Cohorts 1 and 2 in this investigation. This is in accord with the 1971–74 investigation.

The telephone interview questionnaire consisted of 65 questions, each with a choice of three to five previously defined answers. The interviewer did not know the composition of the birth-weight groups. The interviews were carried out between December 1999 and April 2000.

The investigation is based on Aggernæs' theory that there are four fundamental human needs, and that the degree of need fulfilment defines the quality of life:

1. elementary biological needs;

2. need for warm human relationships;

3. need for meaningful occupation;

4. need for differing and exciting experiences.

In addition, Aggernæs separates life quality according to subjective and objective aspects. *Objective life quality* is based on social standards, while *subjective life quality* is based on individual life experiences and preferences.

Results of the investigation

Objective life quality in the VLBW group, who did not have a handicap or chronic illness, was significantly lower that that of the reference group with NBW.

The objective life quality in the corresponding group with LBW was not significantly different from the VLBW and NBW groups.

In the group of 13 with VLBW and 9 with LBW, who additionally had a handicap or a chronic illness, the objective life quality was significantly lower.

There was no difference in the subjective life quality of the group with VLBW and the reference group with NBW.

By comparing the VLBW groups from 1980–82 and 1971–74, it was shown that the objective life quality was apparently improved.

The investigators' conclusions

The group with VLBW had a lower objective life quality than did the reference groups. The difference was, however, no greater than if, in a group of 100 youths of normal birth weight, there would be 25 who scored lower in life quality than does the typical young person with VLBW. There were no differences in the subjective life quality between the groups.

The group with handicap or chronic illness scored lower in both objective and subjective life quality.

Since the first investigation (the cohort from 1971–74), the group with VLBW had improved their life quality, but not to the same extent as the reference groups.

Objective life quality in young Danes has apparently increased during the last eight years.

Other international investigations:

—"Early Intervention in Low Birth Weight Premature Infants: Results at 18 Years of Age for the Infant Health and Development Program" (McCormick et al., 2006);

—"Risks for Low Intellectual Performance Related to Being Born Small for Gestational Age Are Modified by Gestational Age" (Bergvall, Iliadou, Johansson, Tuvermo, & Cnattingius, 2006);

—"Perceptual motor difficulties and their concomitants in six-year-old children born prematurely" (Jongmans, Mercuri, Dubowitz, & Henderson, 1998).

Consensus

A consensus conference was held in Denmark in 1990 (Statens Sundhedsvidenskabelige Forskningsråd, 1991), and one of the conclusions made in the report was:

> We are lacking in investigations of the long-term psycho-social consequences of prematurely born children, their parents, and their siblings. Without such sociological data it is difficult to initiate a public debate that will place practical treatment practices in a health and social-political perspective.

Since 1990 only a few investigations have been carried out in the field, and none of them is wide-ranging.

NOTES

1. ETFOL fem års-undersøgelsen, 2002.
2. A full account of the entire investigation in Danish is available on the Neonatal clinics homepage under Rigshospitalet (www.rh.dk).
3. Efterundersøgelse af børn i 9–10 års-alderen født i Nordjyllands Amt 1988/89.

GLOSSARY

Apgar score: a score arrived at by assessing the condition of a newborn baby in the five areas of heart rate, breathing, skin colour, muscle tone, and reflex response, with 10 points as maximum.

Asphyxia, "lack of pulse": the expression used to describe a lack of oxygen.

Bilirubin: break-down product of haemoglobin in the blood; normally removed by the liver, but in some newborns this does not happen rapidly enough and causes jaundice (*icterus*).

Cerebrospinal fluid: the fluid that circulates in the central nervous system.

Cognitive processes: these involve understanding, interpretation of sense impressions, memory, thinking, and learning.

Cohort: a group with statistical similarities to the investigational group.

CPAP, Continuous Positive Airway Pressure: technical equipment that forces air through the mouth or nose into the child's lungs and this way produces enough pressure to enable the lungs to stay inflated.

Dysphagia ("dys" = poor, "phagein" = eat): the term covers conditions ranging from poor or absent swallowing, sucking and chewing ability to drooling, gagging, and so on; it may be caused by anatomical or neuro-muscular defects as well as by infections.

Dysmaturity, small for date: too low a birth weight in relation to gestational age (birth week).

Encopresis, psychosomatic illness: the child has several instances of involuntary bowel evacuation (min. once a month over three months). If it happens after at least one year of controlled bowel movements, it is a physical expression of the child's mental

215

conflicts (*secondary encopresis*). Diagnosis is carried out on the premise that the child is 4 years old, or that it is developmentally at this level, and that somatic causes for the problem have been eliminated.

Hyperalgesia: a condition of altered perception such that stimuli that would normally induce a trivial discomfort cause significant pain. Hyperalgesia is often a component of a neuropathic pain syndrome.

Infantile autism: radical developmental disturbance—for a diagnosis of infantile autism there must be pronounced deviation within the fields of social connection (deviant behaviour), communication (lack of or delayed development of spoken language), and conspicuous stereotypic movements, like flapping of the hands, hopping in one place, or other meaningless motor-stimulating movements; infantile autism is the most radical form of autism.

Partial epilepsy: form of epilepsy where only a minor part of the brain is involved.

Perception/perceptual: understanding and recognition through use of the senses.

Prothrombin: coagulant—substance that assists in minimizing bleeding.

RDS, respiratory distress syndrome: illness arising as a consequence of immature lung development; causes increasing difficulty in breathing; treated by respirator, CPAP, and/or surfactant.

Reflux: insufficient function of the upper sphincter leading to the stomach.

RS virus, respiratory syncytial virus: "cold" virus characterized by tough secretions, wheezy breathing, and severe cough, which may induce vomiting; the virus cannot be treated, but breathing can be assisted; may result in pneumonia and bronchitis in children under age 3–4.

Serum calcium: the calcium content of the blood; too high a level may result in reduced kidney function.

Surfactant, lung surfactant: a chemical that normally appears in mature lungs. Surfactant keeps the air sacs from collapsing and allows them to inflate with air more easily.

REFERENCES AND BIBLIOGRAPHY

Agerholm, H. (1999). Efterundersøgelse af børn i 9–10 års-alderen født i Nordjyllands Amt 1988/89 [Follow-up investigation of 9–10-year-old children born in North Jutland County 1988/89]. *Danske Fysioterapeuter, Nyt om forskning*, 2: 10–17.

Agerholm, H. (2003). Hold fast i de for tidligt fødte [Hold on to the too-early-born]. *Ergoterapeuten*, 1: 5–9.

Andreassen, M. (2002). Sociallovgivningens muligheder for familier med for tidligt fødte børn [Social legislation possibilities in regard to families of prematurely born children]. *Livsbladet*, 4: 14–17.

Ayres, A. J. (1979). *Sensory Integration and the Child*. Los Angeles, CA: Western Psychological Services.

Bergvall, N., Iliadou, A., Johansson, S., Tuvermo, T., & Cnattingius, S. (2006). Risks for low intellectual performance related to being born small for gestational age are modified by gestational age. *Pediatrics*, 117 (3): e460–467.

Bertelsen, B. (2003). Tænk—at være noget særligt . . . [Just think—to be something special . . .]. *Livsbladet, 3*.

Bowlby, J. (1969–80). *Attachment and Loss, Vols. 1–3*. London: Hogarth Press.

Bowlby, J. (1988). *A Secure Base: Parent–Child Attachment and Healthy Human Development*. New York: Basic Books.

Bräuner, F. (2003). Mad og vitaminer skaber mirakler [Food and vitamins create miracles]. *Naturli, 2*.

Brazelton, T. B. (1992). *Touchpoints: Your Child's Emotional and Behavioral Development*. Reading, MA: Addison-Wesley.

Brock, A. (2000). Kære mor . . . [Dear Mother]. *Livsbladet, 1*.

Brostrøm, S. (2002). Viden er ikke nok—paedagogen maa have sin personlighed med [Knowledge is not enough—the educationalist must bring her personality into it]. *0–14*, 2: 10.

Brummerstedt, E. (2001). Børns søvn [Children's sleep]. *Forældre & fødsel, 6*.

217

Danish National Board of Health (2003). Statistics. Retrived from www .sundhedsstyrelsen.dk.

Dansk Præmatur Forening [The Danish Society for Premature Children] (2002). *Født for tidligt?—til institutioner og dagplejere* [Born too early?—For institutions and day-carers]. Leaflet.

Davis, L., Mohay, H., & Edwards, H. (2003). Mothers' involvement in caring for their premature infants: A historical overview. *Journal of Advanced Nursing, 42* (6): 578–586.

Den Nordiske Forening for Instruktører i Spædbarnsmassage (2001). *Spædbørnsmassage* [Infant massage]. Folder.

Dinesen, S. J., & Greisen, G. (2001). Quality of life in young adults with very low birth weight. *Archives of Diseases in Childhood: Fetal & Neonatal Edition, 85* (November): F165–F169.

Ditlevsen, T. (1955). *Kvindesind* [Woman's mind]. Rev. ed. (1986). *Pigesind og Kvindesind* [Girl's mind and woman's mind]. Copenhagen: Gyldendal, 1986.

Dolto, F. (1982). *Séminaire de psychanalyse d'enfants* (3 vols). Paris: Seuil.

Eliacheff, C. (1997). *À corps et à cris. Être psychanalyste avec les touts-petits* [Raging battles: Psychoanalysing small children]. Paris: Poches Odile Jacob.

Fedderholdt, G. (2002). Mærk din intuition—og følg den! [Note your intuition—and follow it!]. *Livsbladet, 4.*

Fredens, K. (1998). Læring og hukommelse [Learning and memory]. *Kognition & Pædagogik, 29.*

Freltofte, S., & Petersen, V. (2001). *Hjerner på begynderstadiet: Neuropædagogik* [Brains at novice level: Neuro-pedagogy]. Copenhagen: Borgen.

Gardner, H. (1987). Developing the spectrum of human intelligences. *Harvard Educational Review, 57* (2): 187–193.

Goleman, D. (1995). *Emotional Intelligence: Why It Can Matter More Than IQ for Character, Health and Lifelong Achievement.* New York: Bantam Books.

Gram, H. (2001). Stress [Stress]. *Livsbladet, 3.*

Graumann, U. (1995). Den dårlige start der bli'r ved—og ved . . . [The awful beginning which goes on and on]. *Vores Børn, 12.*

Greger, E. (1999). Sandplay. *Nyt Aspekt,* 16 September.

Greisen, G. (1994). Meget for tidligt fødte børn [Very prematurely born children]. *Månedsskrift for Praktisk Lægegerning* (July): 851–860.

Grøndahl, A. (2002). Familierådslagning [Family group conference]. *Børnesygeplejersken, 1.*

Hansen, B. M., Dinesen, J., Hoff, B., & Greisen, G. (2002). Intelligence in preterm children at four years of age as a predictor of school function. *Developmental Medicine & Child Neurology, 44*: 517–521.

Hansen, B. M., Greisen, G., & Mortensen, E. L. (2004). Early nasal continuous positive airway pressure in a cohort of the smallest infants in Denmark: Neurodevelopmental outcome at five years of age. *Acta Paediatrica, 93* (2): 190-195.

Hansen, B. M., Hoff., B., et al. (2004). Perinatal risk factors of adverse outcome in very preterm children: A role of initial treatment of respiratory insufficiency? *Acta Paediatrica, 93* (2): 185–189.

Hansen, E. (1988). *Sygdomme i nervesystemet hos børn* [Diseases of the child's nervous system]. Copenhagen: FADLs Forlag.

Hausner, L. (1998). *Teaching Your Child Concentration: A Playskool Guide.* Washington, DC: LifeLine Press.

Helgeland, I. M. (2002). *Forebyggende arbejde i skolen* [Preventative input at school]. Copenhagen: Psykologisk Forlag.

Hille, E. T. M., den Ouden, A.L., Saigal, S., Wolke, D., Lambert, M., Whitaker, A., Pinto-Martin, J. A., Hoult, L., Meyer, R., Feldman, J. F., Verloove-Vanhorick, S. P., & Paneth, N. (2001). Behavioural problems in children who weigh 1000 g or less at birth in four countries. *The Lancet, 357*: 1641–1643.

Hyld, S. M. (2003). Maries søvnrelaterede problemer [Marie's sleep-related problems]. *Livsbladet, 2.*

Ibsen, K. K., Talbro, A., & Aastrup, D. L. (2000). *Pædiatrisk sygepleje og pædiatri* [Child nursing and pediatrics] (5th edition). Copenhagen: Nyt Nordisk Forlag.

Jackson, K., Ternestedt, B. M., & Schollin, J. (2003). From alienation to familiarity: Experiences of mothers and fathers of preterm infants. *Journal of Advanced Nursing, 43* (2): 120–129.

Jerlang, E., Egeberg, S., Halse, J., Jonassen, A. J., Ringsted, S., & Wedel-Brandt, B. (2002). *Udviklingspsykologiske teorier* [Theories of Psychological Development]. Copenhagen: Gyldendal.

Jerlang, E. & Jerlang, J. (2001). *Psykologisk-pædagogisk opslagsbog* [Psychological-paediatric reference book]. Copenhagen: Gyldendal.

Johansen, P. K. (Ed.) (2002). *Kvalitet i specialpædagogisk bistand til småbørn* [Quality of special preschool education for young children]. Copenhagen: Skolepsykologi.

Jongmans, M. J., Mercuri, E., Dubowitz, L. M. S., & Henderson, S. E. (1998). Perceptual motor difficulties and their concomitants in six-year-old children born prematurely. *Human Movement Science, 17*: 629–654.

Jørgensen, K. K. (1996). *Musikkens 2. virkelighed* [Music's 2nd reality]. Hojbjerg: Bogans Forlag.

Joseph, J. M. (1994). *The Resilient Child. Preparing Today's Youth for To-morrow's World*. New York: Plenum Press.

Juhl, J. (2000). *Smil, vi skal spise* [Smile, we are going to eat.] Copenhagen: Forlaget Apostrof.

Kadesjö, B. (2002). *Børn med koncentrationsvanskeligheder* [Children with difficulties with concentration]. Copenhagen: Psykologisk Forlag.

Kamper, J., Feilberg Jorgensen, N., Jonsbo, F., Pedersen-Bjergaard, L., & Pryds, O. (2004). The Danish national study in infants with extremely low gestational age and birth weight (the ETFOL study): Respiratory morbidity and outcome. *Acta Paediatrica, 93* (2): 225–232.

Kirkebæk, B., Clausen, H., & Storm, K. (1996). *Skrøbelig kontakt—For tidligt fødte og deres samspil med omgivelserne* [Fragile contact—premature children and their interaction with the surroundings]. Copenhagen: Dansk Psykologisk Forlag.

Kromayer, H., Weltzer, H., & Lyberth, N. (1992). *Skal barnet I skole nu? En SPU—en skoleparathedsundersøgelse til brug i daginstitution og børnehaveklasse: Om baggrund og anvendelse* [Should the child go to school now? A test to determine readiness to attend day-care and nursery school: Concerning background and use]. Copenhagen: Dansk Psykologisk Forlag.

Kruuse, E. (1984). *Skoleforløbet for børn med lav fødselsvægt* [School progress for children with low birth weight]. Copenhagen: Dansk Psykologisk Forlag og Forlaget Skolepsykologi.

Larsen, A. (2001). Det kan være meget svært at gå i skole . . . [It can be very hard to go to school . . .]. *Livsbladet, 1.*

Lenchler-Hüberts, L. (2002). Behandling af børn med encoprese [Treatment of children with encoprese]. *Børnesygeplejersken, 3:* 15–18.

Lubetzky, O., & Gilat, I. (2002). Kids born too early may be more fearful as teens. *Death Studies, 26:* 523–543.

Lunsing, R. J., Hadders-Algra, M., Huisjes, H. J., & Touwen, B. C. L. (1992). Minor neurological dysfunction from birth to 12 years: Increase during late school-age. *Developmental Medical Child Neurology, 34:* 399–403.

Mahler, M., Pine, F., & Bergman, A. (1975). *The Psychological Birth of the Human Infant*. London: Hutchinson.

Makani, H., & Makani, J. (2002). Hvad er NLP? [What is NLP?]. *NLP Nyt, 1.*

McCormick, M. C., Brooks-Gunn, J., Buka, S. L., Goldman, J., Yu, J., Salganik, M., Scott, D. T., Bennett, F. C., Kay, L. L., Bernbaum, J. C., Bauer, C. R., Martin, C., Woods, E. R., Martin, A., & Casey, P. H. (2006). Early intervention in low birth weight premature infants:

Results at 18 years of age for the Infant Health and Development Program. *Pediatrics*, 117 (3): 771–780.

Milsted, T. (1999). *Stress*. Copenhagen: Børsens Forlag.

Mogensen, J. (2002). Når psyken former hjernen [When the psyche shapes the brain]. *Psykiatri Information, 3*: 10–11.

Møller, N. (2001). Vi troede vi var dårlige forældre [We thought we were bad parents]. *Børn & Unge, 37*.

The Mother's Help's first group of premature mothers (1996). *Socialpædagogen, 8.*

Nathanielsz, P. W. (1996). *Livet før fødslen—og en tid til at fødes* [Life before birth—and a time to be born]. Copenhagen: Rosinante Munksgaard.

Nielsen, A. (2002). Danske spædbørns sygelighed i de første levemåneder [Danish infants' sickliness during their first months of life]. *Ugeskrift for Læger, 164*: 5644–5648.

Nielsen, J. (1996). *Socialpædagogen, 8*: 4–5.

NSW Health (1998). *Helping Children with Concentration Problems: A Guide to ADD, the Signs and Where to Get Help*. Sydney,: NSW Multicultural Health Communication Service (November).

Obel, C. (2003). *Epidemiological Studies of Stress during Pregnancy and Fetal Brain Development*. Aarhus: Århus Universitets Sundhedsvidenskabelige Fakultet.

Ottosen, M. H., & Bengtsson, T. T. (2002). Et differentieret fællesskab: Om relationer i børnehaver, hvor der er børn med handicap [A differentiated fellowship: About relationships in kindergardens, where there are handicapped children]. *Socialforskningsinstituttet* (February): 24.

Palm, M. (2001). *Raske børn er glade børn* [Healthy children are happy children]. Copenhagen: Klitrose.

Peitersen, B., & Arrøe, M. (1991). *Neonatologi. Det raske og det syge nyfødte barn* [The healthy and the ailing newborn child]. Copenhagen: Nyt Nordisk Forlag Arnold Busck.

Petersen, A. (2001). "At se bag om frygten . . ." [To see what lies behind the fear . . .]. *Livsbladet, 1.*

Riise, S. (1996). *Socialpædagogen, 8*: 4–5

Rogge, J.-U. (1998). *Når børn er bange* [When children are frightened]. Copenhagen: Schønberg.

Rosenberg, T. (2002a). *Hjælp dit barn* [Help your child]. Silkeborg: Forlaget Trine Rosenberg.

Rosenberg, T. (2002b). Kranio-Sakral Terapi til for tidligt fødte børn [Cranio sacral therapy for premature children]. *Liv & Krop, 8.*

Roth, S. C., Baudin, J., Pezzani-Goldsmith, M., Townsend, J., & Reynolds,

E. O. (1994). Relation between neurodevelopmental status of very preterm infants at one and eight years. *Developmental Medical Child Neurology, 36*: 1049–1062.

Rouw, I. (1997). Brug sproget [Use your language]. *Forældre og Børn, 7*: 24–32.

Russell, B. G. (1997). *Dysfagi* [Dysphagia]. Casebook. Copenhagen: Spastikerforeningen.

Schaffer, H. R. (1990). *Making Decisions about Children.* Oxford: Blackwell.

Schledermann, M. (2001). Spis, min pige [Eat, my girl]. *Livsbladet, 1.*

Sørensen, A., Andersen, M., Christiansen, K., Doj, I., Eg, M., Hansen, Aa., Nielsen, L., & Thomsen, H. H. (2001). SIG-neonatalsygeplejegruppen. "Indtryk fra 2. nordiske kongres om børn og smerter" [Impressions from the 2nd Nordic Congress on Children and Pain]. *Børnesygeplejersken, 2*: 27.

Sørensen, A., Andersen, M., Christiansen, K., Doj, I., Eg, M., Hansen, Aa., Nielsen, L., & Thomsen, H. H. (2001). SIG-neonatalsygeplejegruppen. "Smerter hos præmature og syge nyfødte børn" [Pain in premature and ailing newborn children]. *Børnesygeplejersken, 2*: 11–13.

Sørensen, I. (2001). *Børns sygsomme—en helt naturlig løsning* [Children's diseases—a totally natural solution]. Vejle: Forlaget sund & rask.

Statens Sundhedsvidenskabelige Forskningsråd og Dansk Sygepleje Institut (1991). *Ekstremt tidligt fødte børn* [Extremely prematurely born children]. *Konsensus-rapport.* Copenhagen: Statens Sundhedsvidenskabelige Forskningsraad; Dansk Sygepleje Institut.

Stiefenhofer, M. (2002a). *Mit barn kan ikke falde i søvn* [My child will not sleep]. Espergaerde: Lamberths Forlag.

Stiefenhofer, M. (2002b). *Mit barn kan ikke koncentrere sig* [My child cannot concentrate]. Espergaerde: Lamberths Forlag.

Stjernqvist, K. (1996). The birth of an extremely low birth weight infant (ELBW) < 901 g: Impact on the family after 1 and 4 years. *Journal of Reproductive and Infant Psychology, 14*: 243–264.

Stjernqvist, K. (1999). *Född för tidigt* [Born too early]. Stockholm: Natur och Kultur.

Sundhedsstyrelsen (1994). *Neonatologiens fremtidige organisation. Redegørelse* [The future organization of neonatology]. Copenhagen: Komiteen for Sundhedsoplysning.

Svenningsen, S. (1996). *Socialpædagogen, 8*: 4–5.

Tenney, L. (1997). *Children's Herbal Health.* Orem, UT: Woodland Publishing.

Tierra, L. (2000). *A Kid's Herb Book: For Children of All Ages.* San Francisco, CA: Robert D. Reed.

Tóroddsdóttir, T. (2001). *Klodsmajorer og englebørn* [Bumblers and angels]. Copenhagen: Borgens Forlag.

Trillingsgaard, A., Dalby, M. A., & Østergaard, J. R. (2003). *Børn der er anderledes. Hjernens betydning for barnets udvikling* [Children who are different: The brain's significance on the child's development]. Copenhagen: Dansk Psykologisk Forlag.

Tuxen, P., & Filstrup, B. (2002) Ergoterapi som forebyggende indsats i forhold til præmature børn [Ergotherapy as a preventative effort in relation to premature children]. *Livsbladet, 1.*

Ulvund, S. E., Smith, L., & Lindemann, R. (2001). Psykologisk status ved 8–9 års alder hos barn med fødselsvekt under 1501 gram [Psychological status at the age of 8–9 in children of birth weight under 1,501 g]. *Tidsskriftet for Den norske Lægeforening, 121*: 298–302.

Ulvund, S. E., Smith, L., Lindemann, R., & Ulvund, A. (1992). *Lettvektere* [Lighweights]. Oslo: Universitetsforlaget.

Wieben, J. (2001) Marte Meo—samspil med for tidligt fødte børn [Marte Meo—interaction with very premature children]. *Livsbladet 4.*

Zlotnik, G. (2001). Børn og stress [Children and Stress]. *Ugeskrift for Læger, 163* (8): 1121–1124.

Zubrick, S. R., Macartney, H., & Stanley, F. J. (1988). Hidden handicap in school-age children who received neonatal intensive care. *Developmental Medical Child Neurology, 30*: 145–152.

ADDITIONAL RELEVANT LITERATURE AND WEB INFORMATION

Books

Aarts, M. (2000). *Marte Meo: On One's Own Strength.* Harderwijk, The Netherlands: Aarts Productions.

Bradford, V. (2000). *Your Premature Baby, The First Years.* London: Frances Lincoln.

Bradway, K., & McCoard, B. (1997). *Sandplay: Silent Workshop of the Psyche.* London: Routledge.

Bundy, A. C., Lane, S. J., & Murray, E. A. (2002). *Sensory Integration: Theory and Practice.* Philadelphia, PA: F. A. Davis.

Cohen, M. (2003). *Sent Before My Time: A Child Psychotherapist's View of Life on a Neonatal Intensive Care Unit.* Tavistock Clinic Series. London: Karnac.

Dolto, F. (1982). *Séminaire de psychanalyse d'enfants* (3 vols). Paris: Seuil.

Eliacheff, C. (1997). *À corps et à cris. Être psychanalyste avec les touts-petits* [Raging battles: Psychoanalysing small children]. Paris: Poches Odile Jacob.

Hill, G. (1981). *Sandplay Studies: Origins, Theory and Practice.* San Francisco, CA: C. G. Jung Institute.

McFadyen, A. (in press). *Special Care Babies and Their Developing Relationships.* London: Routledge.

Negri, R. (1994). *The Newborn in the Intensive Care Unit: A Neuropsychoanalytic Prevention Model.* London: Karnac.

Ryce-Menuhin, J. (1992). *Jungian Sandplay: The Wonderful Therapy.* London: Routledge

Stern, D. N. (1995). *The Motherhood Constellation: A Unified View of Parent-Infant Psychotherapy.* London: Karnac.

Stern, D. N., & Bruschweiler-Stern, N. (1998). *Birth of a Mother: How the Experience of Motherhood Changes You for Ever.* London: Bloomsbury.

Articles

Upledger, J. E. (1978). The relationship of craniosacral examination findings in grade school children with developmental problems. *Journal of the American Osteopathic Association, 77,* June.

Upledger, J. E. (1980). Cranio therapy proves successful with some DD children. *Advocate,* Jan./Feb.

Upledger, J. E. (1983). Cranio sacral function in brain dysfunction. *Osteopathic Annals,* July.

Upledger, J. E. (1988). The therapeutic value of the craniosacral system. *Massage Therapy Journal,* Winter.

Websites

ADHD:

www.addiss.co.uk
(UK)

www.add-adhd.org
(US)

www.tees.ac.uk/schools/SSSL/cactus/skills.cfm
(The Cactus Clinic, UK Caregivers' Skills Programme for children diagnosed with ADHD/ADD)

Concentration problems:

www.babyandkids.co.uk/Learning/Concentration.asp

www.health.nsw.gov.au/health-public affairs/mhcs/publications/
5065.html

www.huntingtonlearning.com/p-concentration.php

www.mentalhealthproject.com/content.asp?id_Content=1315

www.partnershipforlearning.org/article.asp?ArticleID=473

Cranio-sacral therapy:

www.iahp.com

www.upledger.com

www.wellnessinstitute.net/directory.php

www.worldwidehealthcenter.net/directory-14.html

Developmental delays:

www.akronchildrens.org/cms/site/de312177cf389913/index.html
(complete evaluations and treatment for infants and children—birth to 3 years—who have or are at risk of developmental delays)

Education and care, through effective inspection and regulation:
www.ofsted.gov.uk

Family group conferences:
www.cyf.govt.nz/1254.htm

Family group decision making:
www.americanhumane.org
(on website, look under "Protecting Children", "fgdm")

Family rights group:
www.frg.org.uk

Infant massage training programmes
www.iaim.org.uk/t_training.htm
(UK)
www.iaim-us.com
(US)

Mental fitness, training brains for:
www.corporate-psychology.net

Mother care:
www.bndes.gov.br/english/studies/KangarooMother.pdf

Nutrition and health care:
www.douglaslabs.com

www.herbalremedies.com/herremforchi.html.

Premature babies:
www.austprem.org.au/resources/products.html
(products, Australia)
www.bbc.co.uk/parenting/having_a_baby/birth_specialcare.shtml
(parents' site, BBC)
www.bliss.org.uk
(parents' site, UK)
www.neonatology.org/neo.links.html
(list of websites)
www.premature-infant.com/index.html
(resource for parents and health-care providers)

Public services, benefits, allowances:

www.direct.gov.uk/Bfsl1/BenefitsAndFinancialSupport/Caring_for_
   someone/fs/en
(UK)

Sandplay:

www.sandplay.net

www.sandplay.org

*Social and health services for children with disabilities
or specific health conditions:*

www.cafamily.org.uk/whenyourchild.html
(UK)

Therapy:

www.aft.org.uk/mainpages/links.html
(family, UK)

www.afta.org/resources.html
(family, US)

www.diplomatie.gouv.fr/label_france/ENGLISH/DOSSIER/
   enfance/05.html
(infant)

www.martemeo.com
(Marte Meo)

Toy libraries:

www.ctl.org.uk
(UK)

www.cincinnatichildrens.org/visit/facilities/libraries/toy-library
(US)

www.bsl.org.au/main.asp?PageId=469
(Australia)

www.southburnett.org.au/members/community/netl/index.shtml
(Australia)

INDEX

229